Handbook of Selected Legislation and Other Documents

Handbook of Selected Legislation and Other Documents

Third Edition

THOMSON

WADSWORTH

Australia • Canada • Mexico • Singapore • Spain • United Kingdom • United States

Printed in the United States of America
1 2 3 4 5 6 7 08 07 06 05 04

Printer: Thomson West

ISBN 0-495-00353-0

For more information about our products, contact us at:
Thomson Learning Academic Resource Center
1-800-423-0563

For permission to use material from this text or product, submit a request online at
http://www.thomsonrights.com.
Any additional questions about permissions can be submitted by email to **thomsonrights@thomson.com.**

Thomson Higher Education
10 Davis Drive
Belmont, CA 94002-3098
USA

Asia (including India)
Thomson Learning
5 Shenton Way
#01-01 UIC Building
Singapore 068808

Australia/New Zealand
Thomson Learning Australia
102 Dodds Street
Southbank, Victoria 3006
Australia

Canada
Thomson Nelson
1120 Birchmount Road
Toronto, Ontario M1K 5G4
Canada

UK/Europe/Middle East/Africa
Thomson Learning
High Holborn House
50–51 Bedford Road
London WC1R 4LR
United Kingdom

Latin America
Thomson Learning
Seneca, 53
Colonia Polanco
11560 Mexico
D.F. Mexico

Spain (including Portugal)
Thomson Paraninfo
Calle Magallanes, 25
28015 Madrid, Spain

Table of Contents

Preface

Much of the study of American government involves understanding legislation that has been enacted by the U.S. Congress. In this handbook, we present excerpts of legislation and other important documents to assist you in making better use of the information that you receive in your American government text concerning politics, discrimination laws, and international relationships.

When Congress passes laws, they are collected in a publication titled *United States Statutes at Large*. These laws are ordinarily referred to in their codified form—the form in which they appear in the federal codes. All federal legislation can be found in the *United States Code* (U.S.C.). These references are called citations. The U.S.C. arranges all existing federal laws of a public and permanent nature by subject. Each of the fifty subjects into which the U.S.C. arranges the laws is given a title and a title number. Titles are further subdivided into sections. A citation to the U.S.C. includes title and section numbers. Thus, a reference to the citation "25 U.S.C. Section 2901" means that the legislation can be found in Section 2901 of Title 25.

Federal legislation can run from a few pages to hundreds of pages in length. To conserve space, this handbook contains only certain excerpts from each statute presented—those thought to best illustrate the legislative intent and purpose behind the statute. A series of three asterisks (***) indicates that a portion of the legislation has been omitted. Four asterisks (****) indicate the omission of at least one paragraph.

Selected
Legislation

The Hatch Act of 1939

INTRODUCTION

The Hatch Act of 1939,[1] also known as the Political Activities Act, significantly restrains a political party from influencing, corrupting, or manipulating federal personnel for political advantage. The act targets certain activities, such as a federal employee's management of or active participation in a political campaign for public office. Congressional interest in limiting the civil service employee's participation in politics stems from the premise that partisan federal personnel could erode the fair and efficient disposition of government services. Congress was also concerned with protecting the federal employee from political pressures when he or she sought job advancement, for example. Under the act, the civil servant freely maintains his or her own political beliefs without the fear of job loss or some other form of retribution. By eliminating even the appearance of political influence peddling, the Hatch Act has engendered public confidence in government. Excerpts from the act, as amended in 1993, are shown here.

EXCERPTS

[TITLE 5] PART II—CIVIL SERVICE FUNCTIONS AND RESPONSIBILITIES
****

Section 1502. Influencing Elections; Taking Part in Political Campaigns; Prohibitions; Exceptions

(a) A State or local officer or employee may not—
> (1) use his official authority or influence for the purpose of interfering with or affecting the result of an election or a nomination for office;
> (2) directly or indirectly coerce, attempt to coerce, command, or advise a State or local officer or employee to pay, lend, or contribute anything of value to a party, committee, organization, agency, or person for political purposes; or
> (3) be a candidate for elective office.

(b) A State or local officer or employee retains the right to vote as he chooses and to express his opinions on political subjects and candidates.
****

---

[1]Excerpted provisions are found throughout Title 5, Sections 1302–7327, and Title 18, Sections 594–1918, of the United States Code.

[TITLE 5] PART III—EMPLOYEES
****

Section 7321. Political Participation

It is the policy of the Congress that employees should be encouraged to exercise fully, freely, and without fear of penalty or reprisal, and to the extent not expressly prohibited by law, their right to participate or to refrain from participating in the political processes of the Nation.
****

Section 7323. Political Activity Authorized; Prohibitions

(a) [A]n employee may take an active part in political management or in political campaigns, except an employee may not—

(1) use his official authority or influence for the purpose of interfering with or affecting the result of an election;

(2) knowingly solicit, accept, or receive a political contribution from any person***; or

(3) run for the nomination or as a candidate for election to a partisan political office; or

(4) knowingly solicit or discourage the participation in any political activity of any person who—

(A) has an application for any compensation, grant, contract, ruling, license, permit, or certificate pending before the employing office of such employee; or

(B) is the subject of or a participant in an ongoing audit, investigation, or enforcement action being carried out by the employing office of such employee.
****

Section 7324. Political Activities on Duty; Prohibition

(a) An employee may not engage in political activity—

(1) while the employee is on duty;

(2) in any room or building occupied in the discharge of official duties by an individual employed or holding office in the Government of the United States or any agency or instrumentality thereof;

(3) while wearing a uniform or official insignia identifying the office or position of the employee; or

(4) using any vehicle owned or leased by the Government of the United States or any agency or instrumentality thereof.

(b)

(1) An employee described in paragraph (2) of this subsection may engage in political activity otherwise prohibited by subsection (a) if the costs associated with that political activity are not paid for by money derived from the Treasury of the United States.
****

[TITLE 18] PART I—CRIMES

****

Section 600. Promise of Employment or Other Benefit for Political Activity

Whoever, directly or indirectly, promises any employment, position, compensation, contract, appointment, or other benefit, provided for or made possible in whole or in part by any Act of Congress, or any special consideration in obtaining any such benefit, to any person as consideration, favor, or reward for any political activity or for the support of or opposition to any candidate or any political party in connection with any general or special election to any political office, or in connection with any primary election or political convention or caucus held to select candidates for any political office, shall be fined not more than $10,000 or imprisoned not more than one year, or both.

Section 601. Deprivation of Employment or Other Benefit for Political Contribution

(a) Whoever, directly or indirectly, knowingly causes or attempts to cause any person to make a contribution of a thing of value (including services) for the benefit of any candidate or any political party, by means of the denial or deprivation, or the threat of the denial or deprivation, of—

> (1) any employment, position, or work in or for any agency or other entity of the Government of the United States, a State, or a political subdivision of a State, or any compensation or benefit of such employment, position, or work; or
> (2) any payment or benefit of a program of the United States, a State, or a political subdivision of a State; if such employment, position, work, compensation, payment, or benefit is provided for or made possible in whole or in part by an Act of Congress, shall be fined not more than $10,000, or imprisoned not more than one year, or both.

The Federal Regulation of Lobbying Act of 1946

INTRODUCTION

The Federal Regulation of Lobbying Act of 1946,[2] often referred to as the Legislative Reorganization Act, places stringent disclosure and reporting requirements on lobbyists seeking to influence the federal legislative process. (Excerpts from the act are reproduced below.) The act addresses the risk of harm to the democratic process that could result should a lobby purport to represent a large segment of the general public but, in reality, represents only a small group with a specific political agenda. Although the act does not curtail lobbying activities, it does ensure that the lobbyist's political program is clearly understood by congressional leaders. This is accomplished through the reporting and disclosure requirements of the act (for example, mandatory quarterly reporting for publication in the Congressional Record). Failure to comply with the Lobbying Act's disclosure requirements could result in penalties to the violator, such as a $10,000 fine and imprisonment for up to five years.

EXCERPTS

Section 262. Detailed Accounts of Contributions; Retention of Receipted Bills of Expenditures

(a) It shall be the duty of every person who shall in any manner solicit or receive a contribution to any organization or fund for the purposes hereinafter designated to keep a detailed and exact account of—

(1) all contributions of any amount or of any value whatsoever;
(2) the name and address of every person making any such contribution of $500 or more and the date thereof;
(3) all expenditures made by or on behalf of such organization or fund; and
(4) the name and address of every person to whom any such expenditure is made and the date thereof.
****

Section 263. Receipts for Contributions

Every individual who receives a contribution of $500 or more for any of the purposes hereinafter designated shall within five days after

---

[2]Excerpted provisions are found in Title 2, Sections 261–270, of the United States Code.

5

receipt thereof rendered[3] to the person or organization for which such contribution was received a detailed account thereof, including the name and address of the person making such contribution and the date on which received.

Section 264. Statements of Accounts Filed with Clerk of House
(a) Every person receiving any contributions or expending any money for the purposes designated in subparagraph (a) or (b) of section 266 of this title shall file with the Clerk between the first and tenth day of each calendar quarter, a statement containing complete as of the day next preceding the date of filing—

> (1) the name and address of each person who has made a contribution of $500 or more not mentioned in the preceding report; except that the first report filed pursuant to this chapter shall contain the name and address of each person who has made any contribution of $500 or more to such person since August 2, 1946;
> (2) the total sum of the contributions made to or for such person during the calendar year and not stated under paragraph (1) of this subsection;
> (3) the total sum of all contributions made to or for such person during the calendar year;
> (4) the name and address of each person to whom an expenditure in one or more items of the aggregate amount or value, within the calendar year, of $10 or more has been made by or on behalf of such person, and the amount, date, and purpose of such expenditure;
> (5) the total sum of all expenditures made by or on behalf of such person during the calendar year and not stated under paragraph (4) of this subsection;
> (6) the total sum of expenditures made by or on behalf of such person during the calendar year.

(b) The statements required to be filed by subsection (a) of this section shall be cumulative during the calendar year to which they relate, but where there has been no change in an item reported in a previous statement only the amount need be carried forward.
> ****

Section 266. Persons to Whom Chapter is Applicable
The provisions of this chapter shall apply to any person***who by himself, or through any agent or employee or other persons in any manner whatsoever, directly or indirectly, solicits, collects, or receives money or any other thing of value to be used principally to aid, or the principal purpose of which person is to aid, in the accomplishment of any of the following purposes:
(a) The passage or defeat of any legislation by the Congress of the United States.

---

[3]So in original. Probably should be "render."

(b) To influence, directly or indirectly, the passage or defeat of any legislation by the Congress of the United States.

Section 267. Registration of Lobbyists with Secretary of the Senate and Clerk of House; Compilation of Information

(a) Any person who shall engage himself for pay or for any consideration for the purpose of attempting to influence the passage or defeat of any legislation by the Congress of the United States shall, before doing anything in furtherance of such object, register with the Clerk of the House of Representatives and the Secretary of the Senate and shall give to those officers in writing and under oath, his name and business address, the name and address of the person by whom he is employed, and in whose interest he appears or works, the duration of such employment, how much he is paid and is to receive, by whom he is paid or is to be paid, how much he is to be paid for expenses, and what expenses are to be included. ***

(b) All information required to be filed under the provisions of this section with the Clerk of the House of Representatives and the Secretary of the Senate shall be compiled by said Clerk and Secretary, acting jointly, as soon as practicable after the close of the calendar quarter with respect to which such information is filed and shall be printed in the Congressional Record.

****

Section 269. Penalties and Prohibitions

(a) Any person who violates any of the provisions of this chapter, shall, upon conviction, be guilty of a misdemeanor, and shall be punished by a fine of not more than $5,000 or imprisonment for not more than twelve months, or by both such fine and imprisonment.

(b) In addition to the penalties provided for in subsection (a) of this section, any person convicted of the misdemeanor specified therein is prohibited, for a period of three years from the date of such conviction, from attempting to influence, directly or indirectly, the passage or defeat of any proposed legislation or from appearing before a committee of the Congress in support of or opposition to proposed legislation; and any person who violates any provision of this subsection shall, upon conviction thereof, be guilty of a felony, and shall be punished by a fine of not more than $10,000, or imprisonment for not more than five years, or by both such fine and imprisonment.

Title VII of the Civil Rights Act of 1964

INTRODUCTION

Until the early 1960s, private employers were free to discriminate openly against minorities or any other group. Title VII of the Civil Rights Act of 1964[4] prohibited much of the employment discrimination that was aimed at certain groups because of their race, gender, color, religion, or national origin. (See excerpted provisions.) Only these protected classes are sheltered from discrimination under the act; however, other unlisted groups (such as homosexuals) must seek protection from discrimination elsewhere in the law. The act shelters the protected classes from all significant forms of employment discrimination at any stage of employment. Therefore a business may not discriminate in the screening and hiring of job applicants. An employer may not consider the prohibited factors when firing workers, setting pay scales, or granting promotions. The law also prohibits discrimination regarding the "terms and conditions of employment." This means that an employer cannot expect a given protected class of workers to work longer days or suffer under less desirable working conditions than other employees. The act also created the Equal Employment Opportunity Commission (EEOC) to assist in both the resolution and prosecution of discrimination cases on behalf of affected employees.

EXCERPTS

Section 2000e-1. Foreign and Religious Employment
(a) *Inapplicability of Subchapter to Certain Aliens and Employees of Religious Entities*
This subchapter shall not apply to***a religious corporation, association, educational institution, or society with respect to the employment of individuals of a particular religion to perform work connected with the carrying on by such corporation, association, educational institution, or society of its activities.
   ****

Section 2000e-2. Unlawful Employment Practices
(a) *Employer Practices*
It shall be an unlawful employment practice for an employer—

---

[4]Excerpted provisions are found in Title 42, Sections 2000e–2000e-17, of the United States Code.

> (1) to fail or refuse to hire or to discharge any individual, or otherwise to discriminate against any individual with respect to his compensation, terms, conditions, or privileges of employment, because of such individual's race, color, religion, sex, or national origin; or
> (2) to limit, segregate, or classify his employees or applicants for employment in any way which would deprive or tend to deprive any individual of employment opportunities or otherwise adversely affect his status as an employee, because of such individual's race, color, religion, sex, or national origin.

(b) *Employment Agency Practices*
It shall be an unlawful employment practice for an employment agency to fail or refuse to refer for employment, or otherwise to discriminate against***or to classify or refer for employment any individual on the basis of his race, color, religion, sex, or national origin.

(c) *Labor Organization Practices*
It shall be an unlawful employment practice for a labor organization—

> (1) to exclude or to expel from its membership, or otherwise to discriminate against, any individual because of his race, color, religion, sex, or national origin;
> (2) to limit, segregate, or classify its membership or applicants for membership***in any way which would deprive***any individual of employment opportunities***or otherwise adversely affect his status as an employee or as an applicant for employment, because of such individual's race, color, religion, sex, or national origin; or
> (3) to cause or attempt to cause an employer to discriminate against an individual in violation of this section.

(d) *Training Programs*
It shall be an unlawful employment practice***to discriminate against any individual because of his race, color, religion, sex, or national origin in admission to, or employment in, any program established to provide apprenticeship or other training.

(e) *Businesses or Enterprises with Personnel Qualified on Basis of Religion, Sex, or National Origin; Educational Institutions with Personnel of Particular Religion*
Notwithstanding any other provision of this subchapter,

> (1) it shall not be an unlawful employment practice***to admit or employ any individual***on the basis of his religion, sex, or national origin in those certain instances where religion, sex, or national origin is a bona fide occupational qualification reasonably necessary to the normal operation of that particular business or enterprise[.]***
> ****

(h) *Seniority or Merit System; Quantity or Quality of Production; Ability Tests; Compensation Based on Sex and Authorized by Minimum Wage Provisions*

[I]t shall not be an unlawful employment practice for an employer to apply different standards of compensation, or different terms, conditions, or privileges of employment pursuant to a bona fide seniority or merit system***provided that such differences are not the result of an intention to discriminate because of race, color, religion, sex, or national origin, nor shall it be an unlawful employment practice for an employer to give and to act upon the results of any professionally developed ability test provided that such test, its administration or action upon the results is not designed, intended or used to discriminate because of race, color, religion, sex or national origin.***
        ****

(j) *Preferential Treatment Not to Be Granted on Account of Existing Number or Percentage Imbalance*
Nothing contained in this subchapter shall be interpreted to require***preferential treatment to any individual or to any group because of***race, color, religion, sex, or national origin***.
        ****

Section 2000e-3. Other Unlawful Employment Practices
(a) *Discrimination for Making Charges, Testifying, Assisting, or Participating in Enforcement Proceedings*
It shall be an unlawful employment practice***to discriminate against any individual***because he has opposed any practice made an unlawful employment practice by this subchapter, or because he has made a charge, testified, assisted, or participated in any manner in an investigation, proceeding, or hearing under this subchapter.
(b) *Printing or Publication of Notices or Advertisements Indicating Prohibited Preference, Limitation, Specification, or Discrimination; Occupational Qualification Exception*
It shall be an unlawful employment practice***to print or publish***any notice or advertisement relating to employment***indicating any preference, limitation, specification, or discrimination, based on race, color, religion, sex, or national origin, except***when religion, sex, or national origin is a bona fide occupational qualification for employment.
        ****

Section 2000e-5. Enforcement Provisions
(a) *Power of Commission to Prevent Unlawful Employment Practices*
The [Equal Employment Opportunity] Commission is empowered***to prevent any person from engaging in any unlawful employment practice as set forth in section 2000e-2 or 2000e-3 of this title.
        ****

(g) *Relief Available*
    (1) If the court finds that the respondent has intentionally engaged in***an unlawful employment practice***the court may enjoin the respondent from engaging in such unlawful employment practice, and order such affirmative action as may be appropriate, which may include, but is not limited to, reinstatement or hiring of employees, with or without back

pay***, or any other equitable relief as the court deems appropriate.***

The Voting Rights Act of 1965

INTRODUCTION

The Voting Rights Act of 1965,[5] as amended, ensures that all qualifying U.S. citizens have the opportunity to cast their ballots without interference. The act specifically prohibits the use of literacy tests and poll taxes by political subdivisions as a method of discriminating against certain segments of the voting public. Prior to the act, literacy testing had been implemented in some areas of the country to exclude the uneducated poor and certain ethnic groups, particularly those citizens whose primary language was other than English. The poll tax, which was ordinarily levied against all voters within the political subdivision, was often set sufficiently high to eliminate the low-income vote, yet sufficiently low for middle and high income voters to manage the fee with ease. These screening techniques kept political control in the hands of the establishment, while minority groups and the poor were left underrepresented and politically powerless. To ensure compliance with its provisions, the act gave the Attorney General the authority to assign election observers to ensure that those citizens who qualify and desire to exercise their right to vote are able to do so freely. Some important provisions of the Voting Rights Act are reproduced here.

EXCERPTS

Section 1971. Voting Rights
(a) *Race, Color, or Previous Condition Not to Affect Right to Vote; Uniform Standards for Voting Qualification; Errors or Omissions from Papers; Literacy Tests; Agreements between Attorney General and State or Local Authorities; Definitions*
(1) All citizens of the United States who are otherwise qualified by law to vote at any election by the people in any State, Territory, district, county, city, parish, township, school district, municipality, or other territorial subdivision, shall be entitled and allowed to vote at all such elections, without distinction of race, color, or previous condition of servitude; any constitution, law, custom, usage, or regulation of any State or Territory, or by under its authority, to the contrary notwithstanding.
(2) No person acting under color of law shall—

---

[5]Excerpted provisions are found in Title 42, Sections 1971–1973bb-1, of the United States Code.

(A) in determining whether any individual is qualified under State law or laws to vote in any election, apply any standard, practice, or procedure different from the standards, practices, or procedures applied under such law or laws to other individuals within the same***political subdivision who have been found by State officials to be qualified to vote;

****

(C) employ any literacy test as a qualification for voting in any election unless (i) such test is administered to each individual and is conducted wholly in writing, and (ii) a certified copy of the test and of the answers given by the individual is furnished to him within twenty-five days of the submission of his request ***.

****

Section 1973. Denial or Abridgment of Right to Vote on Account of Race or Color through Voting Qualifications or Prerequisites; Establishment of Violation

(a) No voting qualification or prerequisite to voting or standard practice, or procedure shall be imposed or applied by any State or political subdivision in a manner which results in a denial or abridgment of the right of any citizen of the United States to vote on account of race or color, or in contravention of the guarantees set forth in [this chapter].

****

Section 1973b. Suspension of Use of Tests or Devices in Determining Eligibility to Vote

****

(e) *Completion of Requisite Grade Level of Education in American-Flag Schools in Which Predominant Classroom Language Was Other than English*

****

(2) No person who demonstrates that he has successfully completed the sixth primary grade***shall be denied the right to vote in any Federal, State, or local election because of his inability to read, write, understand, or interpret any matter in the English language, except that in States in which State law provides that a different level of education is presumptive of literacy, he shall demonstrate that he has successfully completed an equivalent level of education***.

****

Section 1973h. Poll Taxes

(a) *Congressional Finding and Declaration of Policy against Enforced Payment of Poll Taxes as Device to Impair Voting Rights*

The Congress finds that the requirement of the payment of a poll tax as a precondition to voting (i) precludes persons of limited means from voting or imposes unreasonable financial hardship upon such persons as a precondition to their exercise of the franchise, (ii) does not bear a reasonable relationship to any legitimate State interest in

the conduct of elections, and (iii) in some areas has the purpose or effect of denying persons the right to vote because of race or color. Upon the basis of these findings, Congress declares that the constitutional right of citizens to vote is denied or abridged in some areas by the requirement of the payment of a poll tax as a precondition to voting.
****

Section 1973i. Prohibited Acts

(a) *Failure or Refusal to Permit Casting or Tabulation of Vote*
No person acting under color of law shall fail or refuse to permit any person to vote who is entitled to vote***or is otherwise qualified to vote, or willfully fail or refuse to tabulate, count, and report such person's vote.

(b) *Intimidation, Threats, or Coercion*
No person, whether acting under color of law or otherwise, shall intimidate, threaten, or coerce, or attempt to intimidate, threaten, or coerce any person for voting or attempting to vote, or intimidate, threaten, or coerce, or attempt to intimidate, threaten, or coerce any person for urging or aiding any person to vote or attempt to vote, or intimidate, threaten, or coerce any person for exercising any powers or duties under***this title.
****

Section 1973j. Civil and Criminal Sanctions

(a) *Depriving or Attempting to Deprive Persons of Secured Rights*
Whoever shall deprive or attempt to deprive any person of any [voting] right secured by [this chapter], shall be fined not more than $5,000, or imprisoned not more than five years, or both.

(b) *Destroying, Defacing, Mutilating, or Altering Ballots or Official Voting Records*
Whoever, within a year following an election in a political subdivision in which an examiner has been appointed (1) destroys, defaces, mutilates, or otherwise alters the marking of a paper ballot which has been cast in such election, or (2) alters any official record of voting in such election tabulated from a voting machine or otherwise, shall be fined not more than $5,000, or imprisoned not more than five years, or both.
****

Section 1973aa. Application of Prohibition to Other States; Definition of "Test or Device"
****

(b) As used in this section, the term "test or device" means any requirement that a person as a prerequisite for voting or registration for voting (1) demonstrate the ability to read, write, understand, or interpret any matter, (2) demonstrate any educational achievement or his knowledge of any particular subject, (3) possess good moral character, or (4) prove his qualifications by the voucher of registered voters or members of any other class.
****

Section 1973aa-2. Judicial Relief; Civil Actions by Attorney General; Three-Judge District Court; Appeal to Supreme Court

Whenever the Attorney General has reason to believe that a State or political subdivision (a) has enacted or is seeking to administer any test or device as a prerequisite to voting in violation of the prohibition contained in section 1973aa of this title, or (b) undertakes to deny the right to vote in any election***, he may institute for the United States, or in the name of the United States, an action in a district court of the United States***for a restraining order, a preliminary or permanent injunction, or such other order as he deems appropriate. An action under this subsection shall be heard and determined by a court of three judges***and any appeal shall be to the Supreme Court.

The Civil Rights Act of 1968

INTRODUCTION

The Civil Rights Act of 1968 was signed by President Lyndon Johnson seven days after the death of the Reverend Martin Luther King, Jr., who was assassinated on April 4, 1968. Included in that act is the Fair Housing Act.[6] All of the federal fair housing laws are currently administered by the Department of Housing and Urban Development (HUD). The 1968 act condemns discrimination on the basis of race, color, religion, national origin, or gender in the sale and rental of most housing in the United States. The act applies regardless of whether the seller or landlord has an express policy of excluding certain persons. In 1988, the act was amended to prohibit discrimination on the basis of mental or physical handicap and on the basis of "family status." The latter includes marital status, pregnancy, and number of children, as well as their ages. The act covers all housing built with federal financial assistance, multiple dwellings having more than four units, single-family homes sold in real estate developments that are not owned by private parties, and any private housing sold or rented by real-estate agents. The proscription against discrimination extends to institutions that provide financing and to real estate brokers, agents, and property owners.

EXCERPTS

Section 3604. Discrimination in the Sale or Rental of Housing and Other Prohibited Practices

[I]t shall be unlawful—
(a) To refuse to sell or rent after the making of a bona fide offer, or to refuse to negotiate for the sale or rental of, or otherwise make unavailable or deny, a dwelling to any person because of race, color, religion, sex, familial status, or national origin.
(b) To discriminate against any person in the terms, conditions, or privileges of sale or rental of a dwelling, or in the provision of services or facilities in connection therewith, because of race, color, religion, sex, familial status, or national origin.
(c) To make, print, or publish, or cause to be made, printed, or published any notice, statement, or advertisement, with respect to the sale or rental of a dwelling that indicates any preference, limitation, or discrimination based on race, color, religion, sex,

---

[6]Excerpted provisions are found in Title 42, Sections 3601–3631, of the United States Code.

handicap, familial status, or national origin, or an intention to make any such preference, limitation, or discrimination.

(d) To represent to any person because of race, color, religion, sex, handicap, familial status, or national origin that any dwelling is not available for inspection, sale, or rental when such dwelling is in fact so available.

(e) For profit, to induce or attempt to induce any person to sell or rent any dwelling by representations regarding the entry or prospective entry into the neighborhood of a person or persons of a particular race, color, religion, sex, handicap, familial status, or national origin.
****

Section 3605. Discrimination in Residential Real Estate-Related Transactions

(a) *In General*

It shall be unlawful for any person or other entity whose business includes engaging in residential real estate-related transactions to discriminate against any person in making available such a transaction, or in the terms or conditions of such a transaction, because of race, color, religion, sex, handicap, familial status, or national origin.

(b) *Definition*

As used in this section, the term "residential real estate-related transaction" means any of the following:

(1) The making or purchasing of loans or providing other financial assistance—

(A) for purchasing, constructing, improving, repairing, or maintaining a dwelling; or

(B) secured by residential real estate.

(2) The selling, brokering, or appraising of residential real property.
****

Section 3611. Subpoenas; Giving of Evidence
****

(c) *Criminal Penalties*

(1) Any person who willfully fails or neglects to attend and testify or to answer any lawful inquiry or to produce records, documents, or other evidence, if it is in such person's power to do so, in obedience to the subpoena or other lawful order***, shall be fined not more than $100,000 or imprisoned not more than one year, or both.

(2) Any person who, with intent thereby to mislead another person in any proceeding under this subchapter—

(A) makes or causes to be made any false entry or statement of fact in any report, account, record, or other document produced pursuant to subpoena or other lawful order***;

(B) willfully neglects or fails to make or to cause to be made full, true, and correct entries in such reports, accounts, records, or other documents; or

(C) willfully mutilates, alters, or by any other means falsifies any documentary evidence;

shall be fined not more than $100,000 or imprisoned not more than one year, or both.
****

Section 3631. Violations; Bodily Injury; Death; Penalties

Whoever, whether or not acting under color of law, by force or threat of force willfully injures, intimidates or interferes with, or attempts to injure, intimidate or interfere with—

(a) any person because of his race, color, religion, sex, handicap***, familial status***, or national origin and because he is or has been selling, purchasing, renting, financing, occupying, or contracting or negotiating for the sale, purchase, rental, financing or occupation of any dwelling, or applying for or participating in any service, organization, or facility relating to the business of selling or renting dwellings; ***
****

shall be fined not more than $1,000, or imprisoned not more than one year, or both; and if bodily injury results shall be fined not more than $10,000, or imprisoned not more than ten years, or both; and if death results shall be subject to imprisonment for any term of years or for life.

The Federal Election Campaign Act of 1971

INTRODUCTION

The Federal Election Campaign Act of 1971,[7] as amended, limits the amounts that may be contributed to the campaigns of candidates for federal elective office, and limits the sources of those contributions as well. Specifically proscribed are certain political contributions from national banks, corporations, and labor unions. The act established the Federal Election Commission to administer the act, and also sets out the Commission's functions, responsibilities, and enforcement powers. Under the act, political campaign committees must register, keep detailed records of their expenditures and sources of funding, and disclose financial information through regular reporting to the Commission (such as the names and addresses of new contributors). Excerpts from the Federal Election Campaign Act are shown here.

EXCERPTS

Section 433. Registration of Political Committees
(a) *Statements of Organizations*
Each authorized campaign committee shall file a statement of organization no later than 10 days after designation[.]***
(b) *Contents of Statements*
The statement of organization of a political committee shall include—
>(1) the name, address, and type of committee;
>(2) the name, address, relationship, and type of any connected organization or affiliated committee;
>(3) the name, address, and position of the custodian of books and accounts of the committee;
>(4) the name and address of the treasurer of the committee;
>(5) if the committee is authorized by a candidate, the name, address, office sought, and party affiliation of the candidate; and
>(6) a listing of all banks, safety deposit boxes, or other depositories used by the committee.
>****

Section 434. Reporting Requirements
(a) *Receipts and Disbursements by Treasurers of Political Committees; Filing Requirements*

---

[7]Excerpted provisions are found in Title 2, Sections 431–455, of the United States Code.

(1) Each treasurer of a political committee shall file reports of receipts and disbursements***. The treasurer shall sign each such report.
****

(b) *Contents of Reports*
Each report under this section shall disclose—
(1) the amount of cash on hand at the beginning of the reporting period;
(2) for the reporting period and the calendar year, the total amount of all receipts[.]***
****

Section 437c. Federal Election Commission
(a) *Establishment; Membership; Term of Office; Vacancies; Qualifications; Compensation; Chairman and Vice Chairman*
(1) There is established a commission to be known as the Federal Election Commission.***
****

(b) *Administration, Enforcement, and Formulation of Policy; Exclusive Jurisdiction of Civil Enforcement; Congressional Authorities or Functions with Respect to Elections for Federal Office*
(1) The Commission shall administer, seek to obtain compliance with, and formulate policy with respect to, this Act***. The Commission shall have exclusive jurisdiction with respect to the civil enforcement of such provisions.
****

Section 437g. Enforcement
(a) *Administrative and Judicial Practice and Procedure*
(1) Any person who believes a violation of this Act***has occurred, may file a complaint with the Commission. Such complaint shall be in writing, signed and sworn to by the person filing such complaint, shall be notarized, and shall be made under penalty of perjury***. Within 5 days after receipt of a complaint, the Commission shall notify, in writing, any person alleged in the complaint to have committed such a violation.***
****

(d) *Penalties; Defenses; Mitigation of Offenses*
(1)
(A) Any person who knowingly and willfully commits a violation of any provision of this Act which involves the making, receiving, or reporting of any contribution or expenditure aggregating $2,000 or more during a calendar year shall be fined, or imprisoned for not more than one year, or both. The amount of this fine shall not exceed the greater of $25,000 or 300 percent of any contribution or expenditure involved in such violation.
****

Section 439a. Use of Contributed Amounts for Certain Purposes

Amounts received by a candidate as contributions that are in excess of any amount necessary to defray his expenditures [may not]***be converted by any person to any personal use***.

Section 441a. Limitations on Contributions and Expenditures
****

(b) *Dollar Limits on Expenditures by Candidates for Office of President of the United States*
(1) No candidate for the office of President of the United States who is eligible***to receive payments from the Secretary of the Treasury may make expenditures in excess of—

> (A) $10,000,000, in the case of a campaign for nomination for election to such office, except the aggregate of expenditures***in any one State shall not exceed the greater of 16 cents multiplied by the voting age population of the State***, or $200,000; or
> (B) $20,000,000 in the case of a campaign for election to such office.
> ****

Section 441e. Contributions by Foreign Nationals

(a) It shall be unlawful for a foreign national directly or through any other person to make any contribution of money or other thing of value, or to promise expressly or impliedly to make any such contribution, in connection with an election to any political office or in connection with any primary election, convention, or caucus held to select candidates for any political office; or for any person to solicit, accept, or receive any such contribution from a foreign national.
****

Section 441f. Contributions in Name of Another Prohibited

No person shall make a contribution in the name of another person or knowingly permit his name to be used to effect such a contribution, and no person shall knowingly accept a contribution made by one person in the name of another person.

Section 441g. Limitation on Contribution of Currency

No person shall make contributions of currency of the United States or currency of any foreign country to or for the benefit of any candidate which, in the aggregate, exceed $100, with respect to any campaign of such candidate for nomination for election, or for election, to Federal office.

Section 441h. Fraudulent Misrepresentation of Campaign Authority

No person who is a candidate for Federal office or an employee or agent of such a candidate shall—

> (1) fraudulently misrepresent himself or any committee or organization under his control as speaking or writing or otherwise acting for or on behalf of any other candidate or political party or employee or agent thereof on a matter which

is damaging to such other candidate or political party or employee or agent thereof; or
(2) willfully and knowingly participate in or conspire to participate in any plan, scheme, or design to violate paragraph (1).

The Privacy Act of 1974

INTRODUCTION

The Privacy Act of 1974,[8] as amended, was enacted to protect the privacy of individuals whose personal records were on file with federal agencies in the regular course of that agency's operation. (For example, confidential personal income information and medical records are often filed with the Social Security Administration as part of an individual's application for medical benefits.) Congress determined that the risk of violating a citizen's privacy increases substantially with the government's expanding use of sophisticated computer technology. To further safeguard the fundamental right to privacy under the U.S. Constitution, Congress set specific guidelines for the collection and dissemination of private information when held by federal agencies. The act protects an individual's privacy right by allowing that person to examine and copy his or her agency file. A request for an amendment or correction to the record can then be made to eliminate an inaccuracy due to misinformation or dated material, for example. If a person's rights under the Privacy Act are intentionally violated or unlawfully restricted, then a civil lawsuit for damages may be brought to redress the harm. Some important excerpts from the act are shown here.

EXCERPTS

Section 552a. Records Maintained on Individuals
(a) *Definitions.*—For purposes of this section—
****

> (4) the term "record" means any item, collection, or grouping of information about an individual that is maintained by an agency, including, but not limited to, his education, financial transactions, medical history, and criminal or employment history and that contains his name, or the identifying number, symbol, or other identifying particular assigned to the individual, such as a finger or voice print or a photograph[.]
> ****

(b) *Conditions of Disclosure.*—No agency shall disclose any record***to any person, or***agency, except pursuant to a written request by***the individual to whom the record pertains, unless disclosure of the record would be—
****

---

[8]Excerpted provisions are found in Title 5, Section 552a, of the United States Code.

(5) to a recipient who has provided the agency with advance adequate written assurance that the record will be used solely as a statistical research or reporting record, and the record is to be transferred in a form that is not individually identifiable;
****

(7) to another agency***under the control of the United States for a civil or criminal law enforcement activity***;

(8) to a person pursuant to a showing of compelling circumstances affecting the health or safety of an individual***;

(9) to either House of Congress***;
****

(11) pursuant to the order of a court of competent jurisdiction; or

(12) to a consumer reporting agency***.
****

(d) *Access to Records.*—Each agency that maintains a system of records shall—

(1) upon request by any individual to gain access to his record***, permit him***to review the record and have a copy made of all or any portion thereof in a form comprehensible to him***;

(2) permit the individual to request amendment of a record pertaining to him***[;]
****

(3) permit the individual who disagrees with the refusal of the agency to amend his record to request a review of such refusal[.]***
****

(e) *Agency Requirements.*—Each agency that maintains a system of records shall—

(1) maintain in its records only such information about an individual as is relevant and necessary to accomplish a purpose of the agency required to be accomplished by statute or by executive order of the President;

(2) [attempt to] collect information***directly from the subject individual when the information may result in adverse determinations about an individual's rights, benefits, and privileges under Federal programs;

(3) inform each individual whom it asks to supply information***—

(A) the authority***[for] the solicitation of the information and whether disclosure of such information is mandatory or voluntary;

(B) the principal purpose***for which the information is intended to be used;

(C) the routine uses which may be made of the information***; and

(D) the effects on him, if any, of not providing all or any part of the requested information;

****

(7) maintain no record describing how any individual exercises rights guaranteed by the First Amendment unless expressly authorized by [law] or by the individual***unless pertinent to***an authorized law enforcement activity; [and]
****

(10) establish appropriate administrative, technical, and physical safeguards to insure the security and confidentiality of records[.]***
****

(g)

(1) *Civil Remedies.*—Whenever any agency
    (A) makes a determination***not to amend an individual's record in accordance with his request, or fails to make such review***; [or]
****

    (D) fails to comply with any other provision of this section***in such a way as to have an adverse effect on an individual,
the individual may bring a civil action against the agency, and the district courts of the United States shall have jurisdiction***.
* ***

(i)

(1) *Criminal Penalties.*—Any officer or employee of an agency [who has access to]***records which contain individually identifiable information[and who]***willfully discloses the material in any manner to any person or agency not entitled to receive it, shall be guilty of a misdemeanor and fined not more than $5,000.
****

(3) Any person who knowingly and willfully requests or obtains any record concerning an individual from an agency under false pretenses shall be guilty of a misdemeanor and fined not more than $5,000.

The Native American Languages Act of 1990

INTRODUCTION

The cultural integrity of the Native American populations living in North America began deteriorating when the first Europeans visited this continent. The gradual erosion of Native American culture continues to this day as evidenced by the Indian population's comparatively depressed economic success, their higher than average death rates, and their historically limited political influence as a group. The federal government's earliest attempts at assimilating Indians into mainstream America endangered the existence of a rich and unique heritage of native language. Recognizing the important role that language plays in the continuity of Native American culture and seeking to reverse the trend of linguistic deterioration, Congress passed the Native American Languages Act of 1990,[9] excerpts of which have been reproduced here.

EXCERPTS

Section 2901. Findings
The Congress finds that—
> (1) the status of the cultures and languages of Native Americans is unique and the United States has the responsibility to act together with Native Americans to ensure the survival of these unique cultures and languages;
> (2) special status is accorded Native Americans in the United States, a status that recognizes distinct cultural and political rights, including the right to continue separate identities;
> (3) the traditional languages of Native Americans are an integral part of their cultures and identities and form the basic medium for the transmission, and thus survival, of Native American cultures, literatures, histories, religions, political institutions, and values;
> ****
> (5) there is a lack of clear, comprehensive, and consistent Federal policy on treatment of Native American languages which has often resulted in acts of suppression and extermination of Native American languages and cultures;

---

[9]Excerpted provisions are found in Title 25, Sections 2901–2906, of the United States Code.

(6) there is convincing evidence that student achievement and performance, community and school pride, and educational opportunity is clearly and directly tied to respect for, and support of, the first language of the child or student;
****

(9) languages are the means of communication for the full range of human experiences and are critical to the survival of cultural and political integrity of any people[.] ***
****

Section 2902. Definitions
For purposes of this chapter—
(1) The term "Native American" means an Indian, Native Hawaiian, or Native American Pacific Islander.
****

(4) The term "Native American Pacific Islander" means any descendent of the aboriginal people of any island in the Pacific Ocean that is a territory or possession of the United States.
****

(6) The term "Native American language" means the historical, traditional languages spoken by Native Americans.
(7) The term "traditional leaders" includes Native Americans who have special expertise in Native American culture and Native American languages.
****

Section 2903. Declaration of Policy
It is the policy of the United States to—
(1) preserve, protect, and promote the rights and freedom of Native Americans to use, practice, and develop Native American languages;
(2) allow exceptions to teacher certification requirements for Federal programs***for instruction in Native American languages when such teacher certification requirements hinder the employment of qualified teachers who teach in Native American languages***;
(3) encourage and support the use of Native American languages as a medium of instruction in order to encourage and support—
(A) Native American language survival,
(B) educational opportunity,
(C) increased student success and performance,
(D) increased student awareness and knowledge of their culture and history, and
(E) increased student and community pride;
*** *

(6) fully recognize the inherent right of Indian tribes and other Native American governing bodies, States, territories, and possessions of the United States to take action on, and give official status to, their Native American languages for the purpose of conducting their own business;

(7) support the granting of comparable proficiency achieved through course work in a Native American language the same academic credit as comparable proficiency achieved through course work in a foreign language, with recognition of such Native American language proficiency by institutions of higher education as fulfilling foreign language entrance or degree requirements; and

(8) encourage all [educational] institutions***to include Native American languages in the curriculum in the same manner as foreign languages***.

Section 2904. No Restrictions

The right of Native Americans to express themselves through the use of Native American languages shall not be restricted in any public proceeding, including publicly supported education programs.

Section 2905. Evaluations

(a) The President shall direct the heads of the various Federal departments, agencies, and instrumentalities to—

(1) evaluate their policies and procedures in consultation with Indian tribes and other Native American governing bodies as well as traditional leaders and educators in order to determine and implement changes needed to bring the policies and procedures into compliance with the provisions of this chapter; [and]
****

(3) evaluate the laws which they administer and make recommendations to the President on amendments needed to bring such laws into compliance with the provisions of this chapter.

The Americans with Disabilities Act of 1990

INTRODUCTION

In 1990, Congress passed the Americans with Disabilities Act (ADA)[10] to assist in the elimination of discrimination against handicapped individuals. As stated in the act, "discrimination against individuals with disabilities persists in such critical areas as employment, housing, public accommodations, education, transportation, health services, voting, and access to public services." The ADA is broadly applicable and affects businesses with as few as fifteen employees. The act prohibits, for example, the questioning of an employee or potential employee about the presence or extent of a disability. It also requires that businesses reasonably accommodate their disabled workers or job applicants (assuming that to do so would not cause the employer an undue hardship). Discrimination is allowed under the act in some circumstances, such as when a worker's condition presents a risk to his or her own safety or to the safety of others on the jobsite. Under those circumstances, an employer may refuse to employ that handicapped worker without violating the act. Some important provisions of the ADA are presented here.

EXCERPTS

Section 12111. Definitions
As used in this subchapter:
****

(8) *Qualified Individual with a Disability*
The term "qualified individual with a disability" means an individual with a disability who, with or without reasonable accommodation, can perform the essential functions of the employment position that such individual holds or desires. [C]onsideration shall be given to the employer's judgment as to what functions of a job are essential***.

(9) *Reasonable Accommodation*
The term "reasonable accommodation" may include—
    (A) making existing facilities used by employees readily
        accessible to and usable by individuals with disabilities; and

---

[10]Excerpted provisions are found in Title 42, Sections 12101–12117, of the United States Code.

(B) job restructuring, part-time or modified work schedules, reassignment to a vacant position, acquisition or modification of equipment or devices, appropriate adjustment or modifications of examinations, training materials or policies, the provision of qualified readers or interpreters, and other similar accommodations for individuals with disabilities.

(10) *Undue Hardship*

(A) *In General*

The term "undue hardship" means an action requiring significant difficulty or expense***.

****

Section 12112. Discrimination

(a) *General Rule*

No covered entity shall discriminate against a qualified individual with a disability***in regard to job application procedures, the hiring, advancement, or discharge of employees, employee compensation, job training, and other terms, conditions, and privileges of employment.

(b) *Construction*

[T]he term "discriminate" includes—

(1) limiting, segregating, or classifying a job applicant or employee in a way that adversely affects [that applicant's or employee's]***opportunities or status***;

(2) participating in a contractual or other arrangement or relationship that has the effect of subjecting a ***qualified applicant or employee with a disability to the discrimination prohibited by this subchapter***;

(3) utilizing standards, criteria, or methods of administration—

(A) that have the effect of discrimination on the basis of disability; ***

** **

(4) excluding or otherwise denying equal jobs or benefits to a qualified individual because of the known disability of an individual with whom the qualified individual is known to have a relationship or association;

(5)

(A) not making reasonable accommodations to the known physical or mental limitations of an otherwise qualified individual with a disability***[, unless] the accommodation would impose an undue hardship on the operation of the business***; or

(B) denying employment opportunities to***an otherwise qualified individual with a disability, if such denial is based on the need of such covered entity to make reasonable accommodation to the physical or mental impairments of the employee or applicant;

(6) using qualification standards, employment tests or other selection criteria that ***tend to screen out an individual with a disability***unless the standard, test or other selection

criteria***is shown to be job-related for the position in question and is consistent with business necessity; and

(7) failing to select and administer tests concerning employment in the most effective manner to ensure that, when such test is administered to a job applicant or employee who has a disability that impairs sensory, manual, or speaking skills, such test results accurately reflect the skills, aptitude, or whatever other factor of such applicant or employee that such test purports to measure, rather than reflecting the impaired***skills of such employee or applicant (except where such skills are the factors that the test purports to measure).
****

Section 12113. Defenses

(a) *In General*

It may be a defense to a charge of discrimination***that an alleged application of qualification standards, tests, or selection criteria that***tend to screen out or otherwise deny a job or benefit to an individual with a disability has been shown to be job-related and consistent with business necessity, and such performance cannot be accomplished by reasonable accommodation***.
****

Section 12115. Posting Notices

Every employer, employment agency, labor organization, or joint labor-management committee covered under this subchapter shall post notices in an accessible format to applicants, employees, and members describing the applicable provisions of this chapter***.
****

Section 12117. Enforcement

(a) *Powers, Remedies, and Procedures*

The powers, remedies, and procedures set forth in [the Civil Rights Act of 1964]***shall be the powers, remedies, and procedures this subchapter provides***concerning employment.

The Civil Rights Act of 1991

INTRODUCTION

The Civil Rights Act of 1991,[11] excerpted below, effectively overruled seven important employment law decisions rendered by the United States Supreme Court during its 1989 and 1991 terms. The Court's line of decisions had progressively limited the rights of those persons challenging employment practices as discriminatory. Having examined this judicial trend, Congress determined that certain modifications to existing antidiscrimination laws were needed to successfully deter unlawful employment practices. These amendments to existing laws were accomplished through the Civil Rights Act of 1991. In Section 3, Congress stated the four primary purposes for the act:

(1) to provide appropriate remedies for intentional discrimination and unlawful harassment in the workplace;

(2) to codify the concepts of "business necessity" and "job related" enunciated by the Supreme Court in *Griggs v. Duke Power Co.*, 401 U.S. 424 (1971), and in the other Supreme Court decisions prior to *Wards Cove Packing Co. v. Atonio*, 490 U.S. 642 (1989);

(3) to confirm statutory authority and provide statutory guidelines for the adjudication of disparate impact suits under title VII of the Civil Rights Act of 1964 * * * ; and

(4) to respond to recent decisions of the Supreme Court by expanding the scope of relevant civil rights statutes in order to provide adequate protection to victims of discrimination.

EXCERPTS

Section 101. Prohibition against All Racial Discrimination in the Making and Enforcement of Contracts.

Section 1977 of the Revised Statutes (42 U.S.C. 1981) is amended—
****

(2) by adding at the end the following new subsections:

(b) For purposes of this section, the term "make and enforce contracts" includes the making, performance, modification, and termination of contracts, and the

---

[11]Excerpted provisions are found in Title 42, Section 1981, of the United States Code.

enjoyment of all benefits, privileges, terms, and conditions of the contractual relationship.

(c) The rights protected by this section are protected against impairment by nongovernmental discrimination and impairment under color of State law.

Section 102. Damages in Cases of Intentional Discrimination.
The Revised Statutes are amended by inserting after section 1977 (42 U.S.C.1981) the following new section:

Section 1977A. Damages in Cases of Intentional Discrimination in Employment.

(a) *Right of Recovery.—*

(1) *Civil Rights.—*In an action brought by a complaining party under section 706 or 717 of the Civil Rights Act of 1964 (42 U.S.C. 2000e-5) against a respondent who engaged in unlawful intentional discrimination (not an employment practice that is unlawful because of its disparate impact) prohibited under section 703, 704, or 717 of the Act (42 U.S.C. 2000e-2 or 2000e-3), and provided that the complaining party cannot recover under section 1977 of the Revised Statutes (42 U.S.C.1981), the complaining party may recover compensatory and punitive damages as allowed in subsection (b), in addition to any relief authorized by section 706(g) of the Civil Rights Act of 1964, from the respondent.

****

(b) *Compensatory and Punitive Damages.—*

(1) *Determination of Punitive Damages.—*A complaining party may recover punitive damages under this section against a respondent (other than a government, government agency or political subdivision) if the complaining party demonstrates that the respondent engaged in a discriminatory practice or discriminatory practices with malice or with reckless indifference to the federally protected rights of an aggrieved individual.

(2) *Exclusions from Compensatory Damages.—*Compensatory damages awarded under this section shall not include backpay, interest on backpay, or any other type of relief authorized under section 706(g) of the Civil Rights Act of 1964.

(3) *Limitations.—*The sum of the amount of compensatory damages awarded under this section for future pecuniary losses, emotional pain, suffering, inconvenience, mental anguish, loss of enjoyment of life, and other nonpecuniary losses, and the amount of punitive damages awarded under this section, shall not exceed, for each complaining party—

(A) in the case of a respondent who has more than 14 and fewer than 101 employees in each of 20 or more calendar weeks in the current or preceding calendar year, $50,000;[and]

****

(D) in the case of a respondent who has more than 500 employees in each of 20 or more calendar weeks in the current or preceding calendar year, $300,000.

****

Section 105. Burden of Proof in Disparate Impact Cases.

(a) Section 703 of the Civil Rights Act of 1964 (42 U.S.C. 2000e-2) is amended by adding***the following new [subsections to 703(k)(1)]:

(A) An unlawful employment practice based on disparate impact is established under this title only if—

(i) a complaining party demonstrates that a respondent uses a particular employment practice that causes a disparate impact on the basis of race, color, religion, sex, or national origin and the respondent fails to demonstrate that the challenged practice is job related for the position in question and consistent with business necessity; or
(ii) the complaining party makes the demonstration described in subparagraph (C) with respect to an alternative employment practice and the respondent refuses to adopt such alternative employment practice.

****

(C) The demonstration referred to by subparagraph (A)(ii) shall be in accordance with the law as it existed on June 4, 1989, with respect to the concept of "alternative employment practice."

****

Section 107. Clarifying Prohibition Against Impermissible Consideration of Race, Color, Religion, Sex, or National Origin in Employment Practices.

(a) *In General.*—Section 703 of the Civil Rights Act of 1964 (42 U.S.C. 2000e-2) (as amended by sections 105 and 106) is further amended by adding at the end the following new subsection:

(m) Except as otherwise provided in this title, an unlawful employment practice is established when the complaining party demonstrates that race, color, religion, sex, or national origin was a motivating factor for any employment practice, even though other factors also motivated the practice.

The North American Free Trade Agreement of 1993

INTRODUCTION

In early 1990, the President of Mexico, Carlos Salinas de Gortari, asked President George Bush for a U.S.-Mexico free trade agreement. This request led to what is now known as the North American Free Trade Agreement (NAFTA) of 1993,[12] excerpts of which are shown below. The NAFTA minimizes barriers to international trade by promoting the free exchange of goods and services among its members: the U.S., Canada, and Mexico. The general purposes of the NAFTA were stated in the preamble. The contracting nations agreed to cooperate fully with each other in the international trade arena; to create a more secure market for their goods and services; to reduce trade distortions and barriers between themselves; to establish trade rules that would be mutually advantageous to them; to improve their competitiveness in the global market; to promote creativity and innovation; to create jobs and improve living standards for their citizens; and to promote sustainable development while ensuring that basic worker rights are enforced.

EXCERPTS

PART ONE: GENERAL PART
Chapter One: Objectives
Article 101: Establishment of the Free Trade Area
The Parties to this Agreement***hereby establish a free trade area.
Article 102: Objectives
1. The objectives of this Agreement***are to: (a) eliminate barriers to trade in, and facilitate the cross-border movement of, goods and services between the territories of the Parties; (b) promote conditions of fair competition in the free trade area; (c) increase substantially investment opportunities in the territories of the Parties; (d) provide adequate and effective protection and enforcement of intellectual property rights in each Party's territory; (e) create effective procedures for the implementation and application of this Agreement, for its joint administration and for the resolution of disputes; and (f) establish a

---

[12]Excerpted provisions are found in Volume 32 of International Legal Materials, Sections 289 and 605 (1993).

framework for further trilateral, regional and multilateral cooperation to expand and enhance the benefits of this Agreement.
****

PART TWO: TRADE IN GOODS
Chapter Three: National Treatment and Market Access for Goods
****

Article 301: National Treatment
1. Each Party shall accord national treatment to the goods of another Party in accordance with Article III of the General Agreement on Tariffs and Trade (GATT)***.
2. [N]ational treatment shall mean, with respect to a state or province, treatment no less favorable than the most favorable treatment accorded by such state or province to any like, directly competitive or substitutable goods, as the case may be, of the Party of which it forms a part.
****

Article 302: Tariff Elimination
1. Except as otherwise provided in this Agreement, no Party may increase any existing customs duty, or adopt any customs duty, on an originating good.
****

Article 316: Consultations and Committee on Trade in Goods
1. The Parties hereby establish a Committee on Trade in Goods, comprising representatives of each Party.
****

3. The Parties shall convene at least once each year***for the purpose of addressing issues related to movement of goods through the Parties' ports of entry.
** **

PART THREE: TECHNICAL BARRIERS TO TRADE
Chapter Nine: Standards-Related Measures
****

Article 904: Basic Rights and Obligations
Right to Take Standards-Related Measures
1. Each Party may***adopt, maintain or apply any standards-related measure, including any such measure relating to safety, the protection of human, animal or plant life or health, the environment or consumers, and any measure to ensure its enforcement or implementation. Such measures include those to prohibit the importation of a good of another Party or the provision of a service by a service provider of another Party that fails to comply with the applicable requirements of those measures or to complete the Party's approval procedures.
****

Unnecessary Obstacles
4. No Party may prepare, adopt, maintain or apply any standards-related measure with a view to or with the effect of creating an unnecessary obstacle to trade between the Parties. An unnecessary obstacle to trade shall not be deemed to be created where: (a) the

demonstrable purpose of the measure is to achieve a legitimate objective; and (b) the measure does not operate to exclude goods of another Party that meet that legitimate objective.
****

PART FIVE: INVESTMENT, SERVICES AND RELATED MATTERS
Chapter Eleven: Investment
SECTION A—INVESTMENT
****

Article 1102: National Treatment
****

2. Each Party shall accord to investments of investors of another Party treatment no less favorable than that it accords, in like circumstances, to investments of its own investors with respect to the establishment, acquisition, expansion, management, conduct, operation, and sale or other disposition of investments.
****

4. For greater certainty, no Party may: (a) impose on an investor of another Party a requirement that a minimum level of equity in an enterprise in the territory of the Party be held by its nationals, other than nominal qualifying shares for directors or incorporators of corporations; or (b) require an investor of another Party, by reason of its nationality, to sell or otherwise dispose of an investment in the territory of the Party.
****

PART SIX: INTELLECTUAL PROPERTY
Chapter Seventeen: Intellectual Property
Article 1701: Nature and Scope of Obligations
1. Each Party shall provide in its territory to the nationals of another Party adequate and effective protection and enforcement of intellectual property rights, while ensuring that measures to enforce intellectual property rights do not themselves become barriers to legitimate trade.
****

Article 1709: Patents
1. Subject to paragraphs 2 and 3, each Party shall make patents available for any inventions, whether products or processes, in all fields of technology, provided that such inventions are new, result from an inventive step and are capable of industrial application. For purposes of this Article, a Party may deem the terms "inventive step" and "capable of industrial application" to be synonymous with the terms "non-obvious" and "useful," respectively.
****

Article 1717: Criminal Procedures and Penalties
1. Each Party shall provide criminal procedures and penalties to be applied at least in cases of willful trademark counterfeiting or copyright piracy on a commercial scale. Each Party shall provide that penalties available include imprisonment or monetary fines, or both, sufficient to provide a deterrent, consistent with the level of penalties applied for crimes of a corresponding gravity.

2. Each Party shall provide that, in appropriate cases, its judicial authorities may order the seizure, forfeiture and destruction of infringing goods and of any materials and implements the predominant use of which has been in the commission of the offense.

The General Agreement on Tariffs and Trade of 1994

INTRODUCTION

The General Agreement on Tariffs and Trade (GATT) of 1994[13] has become the principal instrument for regulating international trade. Originally created in 1947 and effective in 1948, GATT was the first global commercial agreement in history. The agreement is periodically renegotiated through "rounds" to reflect changed circumstances—each of which may continue for a period of years. The Uruguay Round, excerpted below, began in 1987, was finished in 1993, and signed in 1994. Pursuant to that round, GATT will be renamed the *World Trade Organization.* GATT is intended to eliminate trade barriers among nations. Trade barriers come in many forms and include strict prohibitions, quotas, tariffs, and dumping. Tariffs are added taxes on imported goods that translate into higher costs to the purchasers of those goods. Because of the increased cost, consumers are more inclined to purchase less expensive, domestically manufactured goods (which carry no tariff) in lieu of the imported goods. GATT also provides protection against dumping. Dumping occurs when imported goods are priced and sold below their fair market value. (Fair market value is ordinarily determined by the price of those goods in the exporting country.) This makes it difficult for domestic producers to compete fairly with the foreign manufacturer of the dumped product. Under Article I of GATT, each member nation also agrees to treat the other member nations at least as well as a country enjoying its most favored trade relationship status. This granting of most-favored-nation status on other members to the agreement is a basic tenet of GATT.

EXCERPTS

PART I
FINAL ACT EMBODYING THE RESULTS OF THE URUGUAY ROUND OF MULTILATERAL TRADE NEGOTIATIONS

1. Having met in order to conclude the Uruguay Round of Multilateral Trade Negotiations, the representatives of the

---

[13]Excerpted provisions are found in the Final Act Embodying the Results of the Uruguay Round of Multilateral Trade Negotiations, Office of the U.S. Trade Representative, Executive Office of the President, Washington, D.C. (1993).

Governments and of the European Communities, members of the
Trade Negotiations Committee***, *agree* that the Agreement
Establishing the Multilateral Trade Organizationand the Ministerial
Decisions and Declarations***embody the results of their negotiations
and form an integral part of this Final Act.
****

PART II
AGREEMENT ESTABLISHING THE
MULTILATERAL TRADE ORGANIZATION

The *Parties* to this Agreement,

Recognizing that their relations in the field of trade and
economic endeavour should be conducted with a view to raising
standards of living, ensuring full employment and a large and
steadily growing volume of real income and effective demand, and
expanding the production and trade in goods and services, while
allowing for the optimal use of the world's resources in accordance
with the objective of sustainable development, seeking both to protect
and preserve the environment and enhance the means for doing so in
a manner consistent with their respective needs and concerns at
different levels of economic development,

Recognizing further that there is need for positive efforts
designed to ensure that developing countries***secure a share in the
growth in international trade commensurate with the needs of their
economic development,

Being desirous of contributing to these objectives by entering
into reciprocal and mutually advantageous arrangements directed to
the substantial reduction of tariffs and other barriers to trade and to
the elimination of discriminatory treatment in international trade
relations,

Resolved, therefore, to develop an integrated, more viable and
durable multilateral trading system encompassing the General
Agreement on Tariffs and Trade, the results of the past trade
liberalization efforts, and all of the results of the Uruguay Round of
multilateral trade negotiations,

Determined to preserve the basic principles and to further the
objectives underlying this multilateral trading system,

Agree as follows:
****

The Multilateral Trade Organization [MTO] *** is hereby
established.
****

[The] MTO shall facilitate the implementation, administration,
operation, and further the objectives, of this Agreement and of
the Multilateral Trade Agreements, and shall also provide the
framework for the implementation, administration and
operation of the Plurilateral Trade Agreements.
****

[Except] as otherwise provided for under this Agreement or the
Multilateral Trade Agreements, the MTO shall be guided by the

decisions, procedures and customary practices followed by the contracting parties of the GATT 1947 and the bodies established in the framework of the GATT 1947.
****

AGREEMENT ON TEXTILES AND CLOTHING
****

1. Members agree that circumvention by transshipment, rerouting, false declaration concerning country or place of origin, and falsification of official documents, frustrates the implementation of this Agreement to integrate the textiles and clothing sector into the GATT 1994. Accordingly, Members should establish the necessary legal provisions and/or administrative procedures to address and take action against such circumvention. Members further agree that, consistent with their domestic laws and procedures, they will cooperate fully to address problems arising from circumvention.
****

2. Safeguard action may be taken***when, on the basis of a determination by a Member, it is demonstrated that a particular product is being imported into its territory in such increased quantities as to cause serious damage, or actual threat thereof, to the domestic industry producing like and/or directly competitive products. Serious damage or actual threat thereof must demonstrably be caused by such increased quantities in total imports of that product and not by such other factors as technological changes or changes in consumer preference.
****

AGREEMENT ON IMPLEMENTATION OF ARTICLE VI OF GATT 1994
****

2.1 For the purpose of this Agreement a product is to be considered as being dumped, i.e., introduced into the commerce of another country at less than its normal value, if the export price of the product exported from one country to another is less than the comparable price, in the ordinary course of trade, for the like product when destined for consumption in the exporting country.
****

3.5 It must be demonstrated that the dumped imports are***causing injury within the meaning of this Agreement. The demonstration of a causal relationship between the dumped imports and the injury to the domestic industry shall be based on an examination of all relevant evidence before the authorities. The authorities shall also examine any known factors other than the dumped imports which at the same time are injuring the domestic industry, and the injuries caused by these other factors must not be attributed to the dumped imports. Factors which may be relevant in this respect include***the volume and prices of imports not sold at dumping prices, contraction in demand or changes in the patterns of consumption, trade restrictive practices of and competition between the foreign and

domestic producers, developments in technology and the export performance and productivity of the domestic industry.
****

9.2 When an anti-dumping duty is imposed in respect of any product, such anti-dumping duty shall be collected in the appropriate amounts in each case, on a non-discriminatory basis on imports of such product from all sources found to be dumped and causing injury, except as to imports from those sources from which price undertakings under the terms of this Agreement have been accepted. The authorities shall name the supplier or suppliers of the product concerned. If, however, several suppliers from the same country are involved, and it is impracticable to name all of these suppliers, the authorities may name the supplying country concerned. If several suppliers from more than one country are involved, the authorities may name either all the suppliers involved, or, if this is impracticable, all the supplying countries involved.
****

AGREEMENT ON SAFEGUARDS
****

2. A Member may apply a safeguard measure to a product only if that Member has determined***that such product is being imported into its territory in such increased quantities, absolute or relative to domestic production, and under such conditions as to cause or threaten to cause serious injury to the domestic industry that produces like or directly competitive products.
****

12. The total period of application of a safeguard measure including the period of application of any provisional measure, the period of initial application and any extension thereof, shall not exceed eight years.
****

AGREEMENT ON TRADE-RELATED ASPECTS OF INTELLECTUAL PROPERTY RIGHTS, INCLUDING TRADE IN COUNTERFEIT GOODS
****

1. Members shall ensure that enforcement procedures***are available under their national laws so as to permit effective action against any act of infringement of intellectual property rights covered by this Agreement, including expeditious remedies to prevent infringements and remedies which constitute a deterrent to further infringements. These procedures shall be applied in such a manner as to avoid the creation of barriers to legitimate trade and to provide for safeguards against their abuse.

The USA PATRIOT Act

INTRODUCTION

If sending the armed services to Afghanistan and Iraq was the United States' military response to the terrorist attacks of September 11, 2001, then the United and Strengthening America by Providing Appropriate Tools Required to Intercept and Obstruct Terrorism Act of 2001 (USA PATRIOT Act) was the country's legislative reaction. Strongly supported by President George W. Bush, who called it "an essential step in defeating terrorism," the act was passed by large margins in the U.S. Senate (98-1) and the U.S. House of Representatives (356-66) just months after the attacks. Among other provisions, the legislation allows for the indefinite imprisonment without trial of those non-U.S. citizens whom the U.S. Attorney General decides to be a threat to national security. Furthermore, the federal government is not required to inform these prisoners of the reasons for their detention, nor provide them with legal assistance. The USA PATRIOT Act also makes it easier for government officials to investigate possible terrorist activity through wiretapping telephone lines and searching computer records. In addition, it permits law enforcement agencies to search persons and places without first obtaining a warrant, as required by criminal law. Although President Bush insisted that it protects the "constitutional rights of all Americans," many observers have been critical of the USA PATRIOT Act on the grounds that it infringes on civil liberties. In particular, some argue that its search provisions run contrary to the Fourth Amendment, its indefinite detention provisions run contrary to the Fifth Amendment, and its trial rights provisions run contrary to the Sixth Amendment.

EXCERPTS

TITLE II—ENHANCED SURVEILLANCE PROCEDURES
* * * *
Section 203. Authority to Share Criminal Investigative Information
* * * *
(b) AUTHORITY TO SHARE ELECTRONIC, WIRE, AND ORAL INTERCEPTION INFORMATION—

(1) LAW ENFORCEMENT- Section 2517 of title 18, United States Code, is amended by inserting at the end the following:

(6) Any investigative or law enforcement officer, or attorney for the Government, who by any means authorized by this chapter, has obtained knowledge of

the contents of any wire, oral, or electronic communication, or evidence derived therefrom, may disclose such contents to any other Federal law enforcement, intelligence, protective, immigration, national defense, or national security official to the extent that such contents include foreign intelligence or counterintelligence (as defined in section 3 of the National Security Act of 1947 (50 U.S.C. 401a)), or foreign intelligence information (as defined in subsection (19) of section 2510 of this title), to assist the official who is to receive that information in the performance of his official duties. Any Federal official who receives information pursuant to this provision may use that information only as necessary in the conduct of that person's official duties subject to any limitations on the unauthorized disclosure of such information.

* * * *

Section 207. Duration of FISA Surveillance of Non-United States Persons Who Are Agents of a Foreign Power

(a) DURATION-

(1) SURVEILLANCE- Section 105(e)(1) of the Foreign Intelligence Surveillance Act of 1978 (50 U.S.C. 1805(e)(1)) is amended by--

(A) inserting `(A)' after `except that'; and

(B) inserting before the period the following: `, and (B) an order under this Act for a surveillance targeted against an agent of a foreign power, as defined in section 101(b)(1)(A) may be for the period specified in the application or for 120 days, whichever is less'.

(2) PHYSICAL SEARCH- Section 304(d)(1) of the Foreign Intelligence Surveillance Act of 1978 (50 U.S.C. 1824(d)(1)) is amended by--

(A) striking `forty-five' and inserting `90';

(B) inserting `(A)' after `except that'; and

C) inserting before the period the following: `, and (B) an order under this section for a physical search targeted against an agent of a foreign power as defined in section 101(b)(1)(A) may be for the period specified in the application or for 120 days, whichever is less'.

(b) EXTENSION-

(1) IN GENERAL- Section 105(d)(2) of the Foreign Intelligence Surveillance Act of 1978 (50 U.S.C. 1805(d)(2)) is amended by--

(A) inserting `(A)' after `except that'; and

(B) inserting before the period the following: `, and (B) an extension of an order under this Act for a surveillance targeted against an agent of a foreign power as defined in section 101(b)(1)(A) may be for a period not to exceed 1 year'.

* * * *

Section 213. Authority for Delaying Notice for the Execution of a Warrant

Section 3103a of title 18, United States Code, is amended--
 (1) by inserting `(a) IN GENERAL- ' before `In addition'; and
 (2) by adding at the end the following:

> (b) DELAY- With respect to the issuance of any warrant or court order under this section, or any other rule of law, to search for and seize any property or material that constitutes evidence of a criminal offense in violation of the laws of the United States, any notice required, or that may be required, to be given may be delayed if--
>
>> (1) the court finds reasonable cause to believe that providing immediate notification of the execution of the warrant may have an adverse result (as defined in section 2705);
>> (2) the warrant prohibits the seizure of any tangible property, any wire or electronic communication (as defined in section 2510), or, except as expressly provided in chapter 121, any stored wire or electronic information, except where the court finds reasonable necessity for the seizure; and
>> (3) the warrant provides for the giving of such notice within a reasonable period of its execution, which period may thereafter be extended by the court for good cause shown.

Section 214. PEN Register and Trap and Trace Authority under FISA

(a) APPLICATIONS AND ORDERS- Section 402 of the Foreign Intelligence Surveillance Act of 1978 (50 U.S.C. 1842) is amended--

> (1) in subsection (a)(1), by striking `for any investigation to gather foreign intelligence information or information concerning international terrorism' and inserting `for any investigation to obtain foreign intelligence information not concerning a United States person or to protect against international terrorism or clandestine intelligence activities, provided that such investigation of a United States person is not conducted solely upon the basis of activities protected by the first amendment to the Constitution';
> (2) by amending subsection (c)(2) to read as follows:
>
>> (2) a certification by the applicant that the information likely to be obtained is foreign intelligence information not concerning a United States person or is relevant to an ongoing investigation to protect against international terrorism or clandestine intelligence activities, provided that such investigation of a United States person is not conducted solely upon the basis of activities protected by the first amendment to the Constitution.';

* * * *

(b) AUTHORIZATION DURING EMERGENCIES- Section 403 of the Foreign Intelligence Surveillance Act of 1978 (50 U.S.C. 1843) is amended--

    (1) in subsection (a), by striking `foreign intelligence information or information concerning international terrorism' and inserting `foreign intelligence information not concerning a United States person or information to protect against international terrorism or clandestine intelligence activities, provided that such investigation of a United States person is not conducted solely upon the basis of activities protected by the first amendment to the Constitution'; and

    (2) in subsection (b)(1), by striking `foreign intelligence information or information concerning international terrorism' and inserting `foreign intelligence information not concerning a United States person or information to protect against international terrorism or clandestine intelligence activities, provided that such investigation of a United States person is not conducted solely upon the basis of activities protected by the first amendment to the Constitution.

* * * *

TITLE IV—PROTETING THE BORDER
Subtitle B—Enhanced Immigration Provisions
* * * *

Section 412. Mandatory Detention of Suspected Terrorists; Habeas Corpus; Judicial Review

(a) IN GENERAL- The Immigration and Nationality Act (8 U.S.C. 1101 et seq.) is amended by inserting after section 236 the following:

MANDATORY DETENTION OF SUSPECTED TERRORISTS; HABEAS CORPUS; JUDICIAL REVIEW

SEC. 236A. (a) DETENTION OF TERRORIST ALIENS-

    (1) CUSTODY- The Attorney General shall take into custody any alien who is certified under paragraph (3).

    (2) RELEASE- Except as provided in paragraphs (5) and (6), the Attorney General shall maintain custody of such an alien until the alien is removed from the United States. Except as provided in paragraph (6), such custody shall be maintained irrespective of any relief from removal for which the alien may be eligible, or any relief from removal granted the alien, until the Attorney General determines that the alien is no longer an alien who may be certified under paragraph (3). If the alien is finally determined not to be removable, detention pursuant to this subsection shall terminate.

    (3) CERTIFICATION- The Attorney General may certify an alien under this paragraph if the Attorney General has reasonable grounds to believe that the alien--

        (A) is described in section 212(a)(3)(A)(i), 212(a)(3)(A)(iii), 212(a)(3)(B), 237(a)(4)(A)(i), 237(a)(4)(A)(iii), or 237(a)(4)(B); or

(B) is engaged in any other activity that endangers the national security of the United States.

* * * *

(5) COMMENCEMENT OF PROCEEDINGS- The Attorney General shall place an alien detained under paragraph (1) in removal proceedings, or shall charge the alien with a criminal offense, not later than 7 days after the commencement of such detention. If the requirement of the preceding sentence is not satisfied, the Attorney General shall release the alien.

(6) LIMITATION ON INDEFINITE DETENTION- An alien detained solely under paragraph (1) who has not been removed under section 241(a)(1)(A), and whose removal is unlikely in the reasonably foreseeable future, may be detained for additional periods of up to six months only if the release of the alien will threaten the national security of the United States or the safety of the community or any person.

(7) REVIEW OF CERTIFICATION- The Attorney General shall review the certification made under paragraph (3) every 6 months. If the Attorney General determines, in the Attorney General's discretion, that the certification should be revoked, the alien may be released on such conditions as the Attorney General deems appropriate, unless such release is otherwise prohibited by law. The alien may request each 6 months in writing that the Attorney General reconsider the certification and may submit documents or other evidence in support of that request.

* * * *

TITLE VIII—STRENGTHENING THE CRIMINAL LAWS AGAINST TERRORISM

* * * *

SEC. 802. DEFINITION OF DOMESTIC TERRORISM.

(a) DOMESTIC TERRORISM DEFINED- Section 2331 of title 18, United States Code, is amended--

> (1) in paragraph (1)(B)(iii), by striking `by assassination or kidnapping' and inserting `by mass destruction, assassination, or kidnapping';

* * * *

> (4) by adding at the end the following:
>
> (5) the term `domestic terrorism' means activities that--
>> (A) involve acts dangerous to human life that are a violation of the criminal laws of the United States or of any State;
>> (B) appear to be intended--
>> (i) to intimidate or coerce a civilian population;
>> (ii) to influence the policy of a government by intimidation or coercion; or
>> (iii) to affect the conduct of a government by mass destruction, assassination, or kidnapping; and

Bipartisan Campaign Reform Act of 2002

INTRODUCTION

The Bipartisan Campaign Reform Act of 2002 (BCRA) is the latest attempt to control the way funds are spent on political campaigns in this country. The goal of the act was not to overhaul the system of campaign contributions. Rather, its primary purpose was to close several loopholes in existing campaign finance law that had effectively rendered any limitations on contributions useless. The most glaring of these loopholes concerned the widespread use of "soft money," a term that refers to contributions that skirt the legal limits on how much an individual or organization is legally allowed to contribute to a political campaign. Under federal law, these limits restrict the amount that can be given to a "clearly identified candidate" in order to support that candidate's election or his or her opponent's defeat. "Soft money," however could be used on "issue advertising" that cleverly promoted or attacked candidates without specifically mentioning them, as well as other "get-out-the-vote" and "party-building" exercises. During the 2002 election cycle, political parties raised and spent nearly $500 million in "soft money"—more than five times the amount raised and spent in 1992. In the minds of many, the injection of such huge amounts of cash into the political process hurts the credibility of American elections. To restore this credibility, the BCRA completely bans "soft money" donations to national parties and federal officeholders and forbids the broadcast of the supposedly non-partisan "issue ads" mentioned above in the sixty days leading up to federal and state elections.

EXCERPTS

TITLE 1—REDUCTION OF SPECIAL INTEREST INFLUENCE
Section 101. Soft Money of Political Parties
(a) In IN GENERAL. Title III of the Federal Election Campaign Act of 1971 (2 U.S.C. 431 et seq.) is amended by adding at the end the following:
Section 323. Soft Money of Political Parties
(a) NATIONAL COMMITTEES

> (1) IN GENERAL—A national committee of a political party (including a national congressional campaign committee of a political party) may not solicit, receive, or direct to another person a contribution, donation, or transfer of funds or any other thing of value, or spend any funds, that are not subject to the limitations, prohibitions, and reporting requirements of this Act.

(2) APPLICABILITY—The prohibition established by paragraph (1) applies to any such national committee, any officer or agent acting on behalf of such a national committee, and any entity that is directly or indirectly established, financed, maintained, or controlled by such a national committee.

* * * *

(e) FEDERAL CANDITATES

(1) IN GENERAL—A candidate, individual holding Federal office, agent of a candidate or an individual holding Federal office, or an entity directly or indirectly established, financed, maintained or controlled by or acting on behalf of 1 or more candidates or individuals holding Federal office, shall not—

(A) solicit, receive, direct, transfer, or spend funds in connection with an election for Federal office, including funds for any Federal election activity, unless the funds are subject to the limitations, prohibitions, and reporting requirements of this Act; or

(B) solicit, receive, direct, transfer, or spend funds in connection with any election other than an election for Federal office or disburse funds in connection with such an election unless the funds—

(i) are not in excess of the amounts permitted with respect to contributions to candidates and political committees under paragraphs (1), (2), and (3) of section 315(a); and

(ii) are not from sources prohibited by this Act from making contributions in connection with an election for Federal office.

* * * *

(4) PERMITTING CERTAIN SOLICITATIONS—

(A) GENERAL SOLICITATIONS.--Notwithstanding any other provision of this subsection, an individual described in paragraph (1) may make a general solicitation of funds on behalf of any organization that is described in section 501(c) of the Internal Revenue Code of 1986 and exempt from taxation under section 501(a) of such Code (or has submitted an application for determination of tax exempt status under such section) (other than an entity whose principal purpose is to conduct activities described in clauses (i) and (ii) of section 301(20)(A)) where such solicitation does not specify how the funds will or should be spent.

(B) CERTAIN SPECIFIC SOLICITATIONS.--In addition to the general solicitations permitted under subparagraph (A), an individual described in paragraph (1) may make a solicitation explicitly to obtain funds for carrying out the activities described in clauses (i) and (ii) of section 301(20)(A), or for an entity whose principal purpose is to conduct such activities, if--

(i) the solicitation is made only to individuals; and
(ii) the amount solicited from any individual during any calendar year does not exceed $20,000.

* * * *

Section 103. Reporting Requirements

(a) REPORTING REQUIREMENTS—Section 304 of the Federal Election Campaign Act of 1971 (2 U.S.C. 434) is amended by adding at the end the following:

(e) POLITICAL COMMITTEES—

(1) NATIONAL AND CONGRESSIONAL POLITICAL COMMITTEES—The national committee of a political party, any national congressional campaign committee of a political party, and any subordinate committee of either, shall report all receipts and disbursements during the reporting period.

(2) OTHER POLITICAL COMMITTEES TO WHICH SECTION 323 APPLIES.—(

(A) IN GENERAL.--In addition to any other reporting requirements applicable under this Act, a political committee. . . to which section 323(b)(1) applies shall report all receipts and disbursements made for activities described in section 301(20)(A), unless the aggregate amount of such receipts and disbursements during the calendar year is less than $5,000.

(B) SPECIFIC DISCLOSURE BY STATE AND LOCAL PARTIES OF CERTAIN NON-FEDERAL AMOUNTS PERMITTED TO BE SPENT ON FEDERAL ELECTION ACTIVITY.--Each report by a political committee under subparagraph (A) of receipts and disbursements made for activities described in section 301(20)(A) shall include a disclosure of all receipts and disbursements described in section 323(b)(2)(A) and (B).

(3) ITEMIZATION.--If a political committee has receipts or disbursements to which this subsection applies from or to any person aggregating in excess of $200 for any calendar year, the political committee shall separately itemize its reporting for such person in the same manner as required in paragraphs (3)(A), (5), and (6) of subsection (b).

Section 201. Disclosure of Electioneering

DISCLOSURE OF ELECTIONEERING COMMUNICATIONS.

(a) IN GENERAL.--Section 304 of the Federal Election Campaign Act of 1971 (2 U.S.C. 434), as amended by section 103, is amended by adding at the end the following new subsection:

(f) DISCLOSURE OF ELECTIONEERING COMMUNICATIONS.--

(1) STATEMENT REQUIRED.--Every person who makes a disbursement for the direct costs of producing and airing electioneering communications in an aggregate amount in excess of $10,000 during any calendar year shall, within 24 hours of each disclosure date, file with the Commission a

statement containing the information described in paragraph (2).

(2) CONTENTS OF STATEMENT.--Each statement required to be filed under this subsection shall be made under penalty of perjury and shall contain the following information:

(A) The identification of the person making the disbursement, of any person sharing or exercising direction or control over the activities of such person, and of the custodian of the books and accounts of the person making the disbursement.

(B) The principal place of business of the person making the disbursement, if not an individual.

(C) The amount of each disbursement of more than $200 during the period covered by the statement and the identification of the person to whom the disbursement was made.

(D) The elections to which the electioneering communications pertain and the names (if known) of the candidates identified or to be identified.

(E) If the disbursements were paid out of a segregated bank account which consists of funds contributed solely by individuals who are United States citizens or nationals or lawfully admitted for permanent residence... directly to this account for electioneering communications, the names and addresses of all contributors who contributed an aggregate amount of $1,000 or more to that account during the period beginning on the first day of the preceding calendar year and ending on the disclosure date. Nothing in this subparagraph is to be construed as a prohibition on the use of funds in such a segregated account for a purpose other than electioneering communications.

"(F) If the disbursements were paid out of funds not described in subparagraph (E), the names and addresses of all contributors who contributed an aggregate amount of $1,000 or more to the person making the disbursement during the period beginning on the first day of the preceding calendar year and ending on the disclosure date.

(3) ELECTIONEERING COMMUNICATION—For purposes of this subsection:

(A) IN GENERAL—(i) The term 'electioneering communication' means any broadcast, cable, or satellite communication which--

(I) refers to a clearly identified candidate for Federal office;

(II) is made within--

(aa) 60 days before a general, special, or runoff election for the office sought by the candidate; or
(bb) 30 days before a primary or preference election, or a convention or caucus of a political party that has authority to nominate a candidate, for the office sought by the candidate; and

* * * *

Section 313. Use of Contributed Amounts for Certain Purposes

(a) PERMITTED USES—A contribution accepted by a candidate, and any other donation received by an individual as support for activities of the individual as a holder of Federal office, may be used by the candidate or individual—

(1) for otherwise authorized expenditures in connection with the campaign for Federal office of the candidate or individual;
(2) for ordinary and necessary expenses incurred in connection with duties of the individual as a holder of Federal office;
(3) for contributions to an organization described in section 170(c) of the Internal Revenue Code of 1986; or
(4) for transfers, without limitation, to a national, State, or local committee of a political party.

(b) PROHIBITED USE—

(1) IN GENERAL—A contribution or donation described in subsection (a) shall not be converted by any person to personal use.
(2) CONVERSION.--For the purposes of paragraph (1), a contribution or donation shall be considered to be converted to personal use if the contribution or amount is used to fulfill any commitment, obligation, or expense of a person that would exist irrespective of the candidate's election campaign or individual's duties as a holder of Federal office, including—

(A) a home mortgage, rent, or utility payment;
(B) a clothing purchase;
(C) a noncampaign-related automobile expense;
(D) a country club membership;
(E) a vacation or other noncampaign-related trip;
(F) a household food item;
(G) a tuition payment;
(H) admission to a sporting event, concert, theater, or other form of entertainment not associated with an election campaign; and
(I) dues, fees, and other payments to a health club or recreational facility.".

Other Significant Documents

The Magna Carta (1215)

The Magna Carta is the "great charter" of English civil liberties. King John signed it at Runnymede on June 15, 1215. His barons forced him to do so. The document, which is excerpted below, consists of sixty-three clauses, which protect the rights of the church, the feudal lords, the lords' subtenants, and the merchants. Royal privileges, the administration of justice, and the behavior of royal officials are also covered in the document.

John, by the grace of God, king of England, lord of Ireland, duke of Normandy and Aquitaine, count of Anjou, to all his archbishops, bishops, abbots, earls, barons, justiciars, foresters, sheriffs, stewards, servants, and all bailiffs and faithful men, health. . . .

Chapter 1

First, we grant to God, and by this our present charter we confirm, for us and our heirs forever, that the English church be free, and have its rights whole and its liberties unimpaired; . . . We have granted to all free men of our realm, for ourself and our heirs forever, all these underwritten liberties to have and to hold, for themselves and their heirs, from us and our heirs.

Chapter 20

A free man shall not be amerced for a small offense unless according to the measure of the offense, and for a great offense he shall be amerced according to the greatness of the offense, saving his tenement, and the merchant in the same manner, saving his merchandise, and the villain shall be amerced in the same manner, saving his tools of husbandry, if they fall into our mercy, and none of the aforenamed mercies shall be imposed except by the oath of reputable men of the vicinage.

Chapter 21

Earls and barons shall not be amerced but by their equals, and only according to the measure of the offense.

Chapter 28

No constable, or other bailiff of ours, shall take the corn or chattels of anyone, unless he forthwith pays money for them, or can have any respite by the good will of the seller.

Chapter 30

No sheriff or bailiff of ours or any other, shall take horses and carts of any free man for carrying, except by the will of the free man.[14]

Chapter 31

Neither we nor our bailiffs will take any wood for our castles, or other of our works, except by consent of the man whose wood it is.

Chapter 32

We will not hold the lands of those who are convict of felony, except for one year and one day, and then the lands shall be returned to the lords of the fees.

Chapter 38

No bailiff in future shall put anyone to law by his mere word, without trustworthy witnesses brought forward for it.

Chapter 39

No free man shall be seized, or imprisoned, or disseised, or outlawed, or exiled, or injured in any way, nor will we enter on him or send against him except by the lawful judgment of his peers, or by the law of the land.

---

[14]In 1216, the chapter was modified to say that the horses and carts should not be taken unless the owner received a special amount of money. In 1217, a chapter was inserted that prohibited bailiffs from taking carts from the demesne of a cleric, a knight, or a lady. In 1225, Chapters 30 and 31 from the Charter of 1215 and the new chapter were combined into a single chapter.

Chapter 40

We will sell to no one, or deny to no one, or put off right or justice.

Chapter 41

All merchants shall have safe conduct and security to go out of England or come into England, and to stay in, and go through England, both by land and water, for buying or selling, without any evil tolls, by old and right customs, except in time of war; and if they be of the land at war against us, and if such shall be found in our land, at the beginning of war, they shall be attached without loss of person or property, until it be known by us or our chief justiciar how the merchants of our land are treated who are found then in the land at war with us; and if ours be safe there, others shall be safe here.[15]

Chapter 46

All barons who have founded abbeys, whence they have charters of the kings of England, or ancient tenure, shall have their custody while vacant, as they ought to have it.

Chapter 53

We will have the same respite, and in the same way, about exhibiting justice of deforesting or maintaining the forests, which Henry our father, or Richard our brother afforested, and of the wardship of the lands which are of another's fee, of which thing we have hitherto had the wardship, by reason of the fee, because someone held of us by military service, and of the abbeys which were founded on the fee of another than our own, in which the lord of the fee says he has the right; and when we return, or if we stay from our journey, we will afford full justice to those who complain of these things.

Chapter 54

No one shall be seized or imprisoned for the appeal of a women about the death of any other man but her husband.

---

[15]In 1216, the words "unless formerly they have been publicly prohibited" were inserted after "All merchants."

Chapter 60

All these aforesaid customs and liberties which we have granted to be held in our realm, as far as belongs to us, towards our own, all in our realm, both clergy and lay, shall observe, as far as belongs to them, towards their own.

Chapter 63

Wherefore we will and firmly order that the English church should be free, and that the men of our realm should have and hold all the aforenamed liberties, rights, and grants, well and in peace, freely and quietly, fully and completely, for them and their heirs, from us and our heirs, in all things and places, forever, as is aforesaid. It is sworn both by us, and on the part of the barons, that all these aforesaid shall be kept in good faith and without ill meaning. Witnesses, the abovenamed and many others. Given by our hand, in the meadow which is called Runnymede, between Windsor and Staines, on the fifteenth day of June, in the seventeenth year of our reign.

Source: William Stubbs, ed., *A Translation of Such Documents as Are Unpublished in Dr. Stubbs' Select Charters* (n.d.), pp. 187–197.

The Mayflower Compact (1620)

INTRODUCTION

The Mayflower Compact was entered into by the adult male Pilgrims in the cabin of the *Mayflower* on November 11, 1620. The forty-one men who signed it agreed to establish a preliminary government. The compact bound the signers to a government by majority rule during the time they knew they had to wait for a royal charter. Many view this compact as the first step in the development of democracy in America.

EXCERPTS

IN the Name of God, Amen. We, whose names are underwritten, the Loyal Subjects of our dread Sovereign Lord King James, by the Grace of God, of Great Britain[,] France[,] and Ireland, King Defender of the Faith, & c. Having undertaken for the Glory of God, and Advancement of the Christian Faith, and the Honour of our King and Country, a Voyage to plant the first colony in the northern Parts of Virginia; Do by these Presents, solemnly and mutually, in the Presence of God and one another, covenant and combine ourselves together into a civil Body Politick, for our better Ordering and Preservation, and Furtherance of the Ends aforesaid: And by Virtue hereof do enact, constitute, and frame, such just and equal Laws, Ordinances, Acts, Constitutions, and Officers, from time to time, as shall be thought most meet and convenient for the general Good of the Colony; unto which we promise all due Submission and Obedience. IN WITNESS whereof we have hereunto subscribed our names at Cape-Cod the eleventh of November, in the Reign of our Sovereign Lord King James, of England, France, and Ireland, the eighteenth, and of Scotland, the fifty-fourth, Anno Domini, 1620.

Mr.	John Carver		Digery Priest
Mr.	William Bradford		Thomas Williams
Mr.	Edward Winslow		Gilbert Winslow
Mr.	William Brewster		Edmund Margesson
	Isaac Allerton		Peter Brown
	Miles Standish		Richard Bitteridge
	John Alden		George Soule
	John Turner		Edward Tilly
	Francis Eaton		John Tilly
	James Chilton		Francis Cooke

	John Craxton		Thomas Rogers
	John Billington		Thomas Tinker
	Joses Fletcher		John Ridgdale
	John Goodman		Edward Fuller
Mr.	Samuel Fuller		Richard Clark
Mr.	Christopher Martin		Richard Gardiner
Mr.	William Mullins	Mr.	John Allerton
Mr.	William White		Thomas English
Mr.	Richard Warren		Edward Doten
	John Howland		Edward Liester
Mr.	Steven Hopkins		

Articles of Confederation (1781–1789)

The Articles of Confederation were in effect the first constitution of the United States, formally joining all the colonies under a centralized government. They were submitted to the Continental Congress in 1776, adopted the next year, but not ratified by all the states until 1781. They remained in force until the ratification of the U.S. Constitution in 1789.

To all to whom these Presents shall come, we the undersigned Delegates of the States affixed to our Names send greeting

Whereas the Delegates of the United States of America in Congress assembled did on the fifteenth day of November in the Year of our Lord One Thousand Seven Hundred and Seventy-seven, and in the Second Year of the Independence of America agree to certain articles of Confederation and perpetual Union between the States of New Hampshire, Massachusetts-bay, Rhode-island, and Providence Plantations, Connecticut, New York, New Jersey, Pennsylvania, Delaware, Maryland, Virginia, North-Carolina, South-Carolina and Georgia in the Words following, viz.

Articles of Confederation and perpetual Union between the States of Newhampshire, Massachusetts-bay, Rhodeisland and Providence Plantations, Connecticut, New-York, New-Jersey, Pennsylvania, Delaware, Maryland, Virginia, North-Carolina, South-Carolina and Georgia.

Article I

The stile of this confederacy shall be "The United States of America."

Article II

Each State retains its sovereignty, freedom and independence, and every power, jurisdiction and right, which is not by this confederation expressly delegated to the United States, in Congress assembled.

Article III

The said States hereby severally enter into a firm league of friendship with each other, for their common defense, the security of their liberties, and their mutual and general welfare, binding themselves to assist each other, against all force offered to, or attacks made upon them, or any of them, on account of religion, sovereignty trade or any other pretence whatever.

Article IV

The better to secure and perpetuate mutual friendship and intercourse among the people of the different States in this Union, the free inhabitants of each of these States, paupers, vagabonds and fugitives from justice excepted, shall be entitled to all privileges and immunities of free citizens in the several States; and the people of each State shall have free ingress and regress to and from any other State, and shall enjoy therein all the privileges of trade and commerce, subject to the same duties, impositions and restrictions as the inhabitants thereof respectively, provided that such restrictions shall not exceed so far as to prevent the removal of property imported into any State, to any other State of which the owner is an inhabitant; provided also that no imposition, duties or restriction shall be laid by any State, on the property of the United States, or either of them.

If any person guilty of, or charged with treason, felony, or other high misdemeanor in any State, shall flee from justice, and be found in any of the United States, he shall upon demand of the Governor or Executive power, of the State from which he fled, be delivered up and removed to the State having jurisdiction of his offense.

Full faith and credit shall be given in each of these States to the records, acts and judicial proceedings to the courts and magistrates of every other State.

Article V

For the more convenient management of the general interests of the United States, delegates shall be annually appointed in such manner as the legislature of each State shall direct, to meet in Congress on the first Monday in November, in every year, with a power reserved to each State, to recall its delegates, or any of them, at any time within the year, and to send others in their stead, for the remainder of the year.

No State shall be represented in Congress by less than two, nor by more than seven members; and no person shall be capable of being a delegate for more than three years in any term of six years; nor shall any person, being a delegate, be capable of holding any office under the United States, for which he, or another for his benefit receives any salary, fees or emolument of any kind.

Each state shall maintain its own delegates in a meeting of the States, and while they act as members of the committee of the States.

In determining questions in the United States, in Congress assembled, each State shall have one vote.

Freedom of speech and debate in Congress shall not be impeached or questioned in any court, or place out of Congress, and the members of Congress shall be protected in their persons from arrests and imprisonments, during the time of their going to and from, and attendance on Congress, except for treason, felony, or breach of the peace.

Article VI

No State without the consent of the United States in Congress assembled, shall send any embassy to, or receive any embassy from, or enter into any conference, agreement, alliance or treaty with any king, prince or state; nor shall any person holding any office or profit or trust under the United States, or any of them, accept of any present, emolument, office or title of any kind whatever from any king, prince or foreign state; nor shall the United States in Congress assembled or any of them, grant any title of nobility.

No two or more States shall enter into any treaty, confederation or alliance whatever between them, without the consent of the United States in Congress assembled, specifying accurately the purposes for which the same is to be entered into, and how long it shall continue.

No State shall lay any imposts or duties, which may interfere with any stipulations in treaties, entered into by the United States in Congress assembled, with any king, prince or state, in pursuance of any treaties already proposed by Congress, to the courts of France and Spain.

No vessels of war shall be kept up in time of peace by any State, except such number only, as shall be deemed necessary by the United States in Congress assembled, for the defence of such State, or its trade; nor shall any body of forces be kept up by any State, in time of peace, except such number only, as in the judgement of the United States, in Congress assembled, shall be deemed requisite to garrison the forts necessary for the defence of such State; but every State shall always keep up a well regulated and disciplined militia, sufficiently armed and accoutered, and shall provide and constantly have ready for use, in public stores, a due number of field pieces and tents, and a proper quantity of arms, ammunition and camp equipage.

No State shall engage in any way without the consent of the United States in Congress assembled, unless such State be actually invaded by enemies, or shall have received certain advice of a resolution being formed by some nation of Indians to invade such State, and the danger is so imminent as not to admit of a delay, till the United States in Congress assembled can be consulted: nor shall any State grant commissions to any ships or vessels of war, nor letters of marque or reprisal, except it be after a declaration of war by the United States in Congress assembled, and then only against the kingdom or state and the subject thereof, against which war has been so declared and under such regulations as shall be established by the United States in Congress assembled, unless such State be infested by pirates, in which case vessels of war may be fitted out for that occasion, and kept so long as the danger shall continue, or until the United States in Congress assembled shall determine otherwise.

Article VII

When land-forces are raised by any State for the common defence, all officers of or under the rank of colonel, shall be appointed by the Legislature of each State respectively by whom such forces shall be raised, or in such manner as such State shall direct, and all vacancies shall be filled up by the State which first made the appointment.

Article VIII

All charges of war, and all other expenses that shall be incurred for the common defence or general welfare, and allowed by the United States in Congress assembled, shall be defrayed out of a common treasury, which shall be supplied by the several States, in proportion to the value of all land within each State, granted to or surveyed for any person, as such land and the buildings and improvements thereon shall be estimated according to such mode as the United States in Congress assembled, shall from time to time direct and appoint.

The taxes for paying that proportion shall be laid and levied by the authority and direction of the Legislatures of the several States within the time agreed upon by the United States in Congress Assembled.

Article IX

The United States in Congress assembled, shall have the sole and exclusive right and power of determining on peace and war, except in the cases mentioned in the sixth article—of sending and receiving ambassadors—entering into treaties and alliances, provided that no treaty of commerce shall be made whereby the legislative power of the respective States shall be restrained from imposing such imposts and duties on foreigners, as their own people are subjected to, or from prohibiting the exportation or importation of any species of goods or commodities whatsoever—of establishing rules for deciding in all cases, what captures on land or water shall be legal, and in what manner prizes taken by land or naval forces in the service of the United States shall be divided or appropriated—of granting letters of marque and reprisal in times of peace—appointing courts for trial of piracies and felonies committed on the high seas and establishing courts for receiving and determining finally appeals in all cases of captures, provided that no member of Congress shall be appointed a judge of any of the said courts.

The United States in Congress assembled shall also be the last resort on appeal in all disputes and differences now subsisting or that hereafter may arise between two or more States concerning boundary, jurisdiction or any other cause whatever; which authority shall always be exercised in the manner following. Whenever the legislative or executive authority or lawful agent of any State in controversy with another shall present a petition to Congress, stating the matter in question and praying for a hearing, notice thereof shall be given by order of Congress to the legislative or executive authority of the other State in controversy, and a day assigned for the appearance of the parties by their lawful agents, who shall then be directed to appoint by joint consent, commissioners or judges to constitute a court for hearing and determining the matter in question: but if they cannot agree, Congress shall name three persons out of each of the United States, and from the list of such persons each party shall alternately strike out one, the petitioners beginning, until the number shall be reduced to thirteen; and from that number not less than seven, nor more than nine names as Congress shall direct, shall, in the presence of Congress be drawn out by lot, and the persons whose names shall be so drawn or any five of them, shall be commissioners or judges, to hear and finally determine the controversy, so always as a major part of the judges who shall hear the cause shall agree in the determination: and if either party shall neglect to attend at the day appointed, without showing reasons, which Congress shall judge sufficient, or being present shall refuse to strike, the Congress shall proceed to nominate three persons out of each State, and the Secretary of Congress shall strike in behalf of such party absent or refusing; and the judgment and sentence of the court to be appointed, in the manner before prescribed, shall be final and conclusive; and if any of the parties shall refuse to submit to the authority of such court, or to appear or defend their claim or cause, the court shall nevertheless proceed to pronounce sentence, or judgment, which shall in like manner be final and decisive, the judgment or sentence and other proceedings being in either case transmitted to Congress, and lodged among the acts of Congress for the security of the parties concerned: provided that every commissioner, before he sits in judgment, shall take an oath to be administered by one of the judges of the supreme court of the State where the cause shall be tried, ``well and truly to hear and determine the matter in question, according to the best of his judgment, without favour, affection or hope of reward:" provided also that no State shall be deprived of territory for the benefit of the United States.

All controversies concerning the private right of soil claimed under different grants of two or more States, whose jurisdiction as they may respect such lands, and the States which passed such grants are adjusted, the said grants or either of them being at the same time claimed to have originated antecedent to such settlement of jurisdiction, shall on the petition of either party to the Congress of the United States, be finally determined as near as may be in the same manner as is before prescribed for deciding disputes respecting territorial jurisdiction between different States.

The United States in Congress assembled shall also have the sole and exclusive right and power of regulating the alloy and value of coin struck by their own authority, or by that of the respective States.—fixing the standard of weights and measures throughout the United States.—regulating the trade and managing all affairs with the Indians, not members of any of the States, provided that the legislative right of any State within its own limits be not infringed or violated—establishing and regulating post-offices from one State to another, throughout all the United States, and exacting such postage on the papers passing thro' the same as may be requisite to defray the expenses of the said office—appointing all officers of the land forces, in the service of the United States, excepting regimental officers—appointing all the officers of the naval forces, and commissioning all officers whatever in the service of the United States—making rules for the government and regulation of the said land and naval forces, and directing their operations.

The United States in Congress assembled shall have authority to appoint a committee, to sit in the recess of Congress, to be denominated ``a Committee of the States,'' and to consist of one delegate from each State; and to appoint such other committees and civil officers as may be necessary for managing the general affairs of the United States under their direction—to appoint one of their number to preside, provided that no person be allowed to serve in the office of president more than one year in any term of three years; to ascertain the necessary sums of money to be raised for the service of the United States, and to appropriate and apply the same for defraying the public expenses—to borrow money or emit bills on the credit of the United States transmitting every half year to the respective States an account of the sums of money so borrowed or emitted,—to build and equip a navy—to agree upon the number of land forces, and to make requisitions from each State for its quota, in proportion to the number of white inhabitants in such State; which requisition shall be binding, and thereupon the Legislature of each State shall appoint the regimental officers, raise the men and cloath, arm and equip them in a soldier like manner, at the expense of the United States; and the officers and men so cloathed, armed and equipped shall march to the place appointed, and within the time agreed on by the United States in Congress assembled; but if the

United States in Congress assembled shall, on consideration of circumstances judge proper that any State should not raise men, or should raise a smaller number than its quota, and that any other State should raise a greater number of men than the quota thereof, such extra number shall be raised, officered, cloathed, armed and equipped in the same manner as the quota of such State, unless the legislature of such State shall judge that such extra number cannot be safely spared out of the same, in which case they shall raise officer, cloath, arm and equip as many of such extra number as they judge can be safely spared. And the officers and men so cloathed, armed, and equipped, shall march to the place appointed, and within the time agreed on by the United States in Congress assembled.

The United States in Congress assembled shall never engage in a war, nor grant letters of marque and reprisal in time of peace, nor enter into any treaties or alliances, nor coin money, nor regulate the value thereof, nor ascertain the sums and expenses necessary for the defence and welfare of the United States, or any of them, nor emit bills, nor borrow money on the credit of the United States, nor appropriate money, nor agree upon the number of vessels of war, to be built or purchased, or the number of land or sea forces to be raised, nor appoint a commander in chief of the army or navy, unless nine States assent to the same: nor shall a question on any other point, except for adjourning from day to day be determined, unless by the votes of a majority of the United States in Congress assembled.

The Congress of the United States shall have power to adjourn to any time within the year, and to any place within the United States, so that no period of adjournment be for a longer duration than the space of six months, and shall publish the journal of their proceedings monthly, except such parts thereof relating to treaties, alliances or military operations, as in their judgment require secrecy; and the yeas and nays of the delegates of each State on any question shall be entered on the journal, when it is desired by any delegate; and the delegates of a State, or any of them, at his or her request shall be furnished with a transcript of the said Journal, except such parts as are above excepted, to lay before the Legislatures of the several States.

Article X

The committee of the States, or any nine of them, shall be authorized to execute in the recess of Congress, such of the powers of Congress as the United States in Congress assembled, by the consent of nine States, shall from time to time think expedient to vest them with; provided that no power be delegated to the said committee, for the exercise of which, by the articles of confederation, the voice of nine States in the Congress of the United States assembled is requisite.

Article XI

Canada acceding to this confederation, and joining in the measures of the United States, shall be admitted into, and entitled to all the advantages of this Union: but no other colony shall be admitted into the same, unless such admission be agreed to by nine States.

Article XII

All bills of credit emitted, monies borrowed and debts contracted by, or under the authority of Congress, before the assembling of the United States, in pursuance of the present confederation, shall be deemed and considered as a charge against the United States, for payment and satisfaction whereof the said United States, and the public faith are hereby solemnly pledged.

Article XIII

Every State shall abide by the determinations of the United States in Congress assembled, on all questions which by this confederation are submitted to them. And the articles of this confederation shall be inviolably observed by every State, and the Union shall be perpetual; nor shall any alteration at any time hereafter be made in any of them; unless such alteration be agreed to in a Congress of the United States, and be afterwards confirmed by the Legislatures of every State.

And whereas it has pleased the Great Governor of the world to incline the hearts of the Legislatures we respectively represent in Congress, to approve of, and to authorize us to ratify the said articles of confederation and perpetual union. Know ye that we the undersigned delegates, by virture of the power and authority to us given for that purpose, do by these presents, in the name and in behalf of our respective constituents, fully and entirely ratify and confirm each and every of the said articles of confederation and perpetual union, and all and singular the matters and things therein contained: and we do further solemnly plight and engage the faith of our respective constituents, that they shall abide by the determinations of the United States in Congress assembled, on all questions, which by the said confederation are submitted to them. And that the articles thereof shall be inviolably observed by the States we re[s]pectively represent, and that the Union shall be perpetual.

In witness whereof we have hereunto set our hands in Congress.

Done at Philadelphia in the State of Pennsylvania the ninth day of July in the year of our Lord one thousand seven hundred and seventy-eight, and in the third year of the independence of America.

On the part and behalf of the State of New Hampshire

JOSIAH BARTLETT,   JOHN WENTWORTH, Junr.,
                         August 8th, 1778.

On the part and behalf of the State of Massachusetts Bay

JOHN HANCOCK,   FRANCIS DANA,
SAMUEL ADAMS,   JAMES LOVELL,
ELBRIDGE GERRY,   SAMUEL HOLTEN.

On the part and behalf of the State of Rhode Island and
Providence Plantations

WILLIAM ELLERY,   JOHN COLLINS.
HENRY MARCHANT,

On the part and behalf of the State of Connecticut

ROGER SHERMAN,   TITUS HOSMER,
SAMUEL HUNTINGTON,ANDREW ADAMS.
OLIVER WOLCOTT,

On the part and behalf of the State of New York

JAS. DUANE,   WM. DUER,
FRA. LEWIS,   GOUV. MORRIS.

On the part and in behalf of the State of New Jersey,
Novr. 26, 1778

JNO. WITHERSPOON,   NATHL. SCUDDER.

On the part and behalf of the State of Pennsylvania

ROBT. MORRIS,   WILLIAM CLINGAN,
DANIEL ROBERDEAU,   JOSEPH REED,
JONA. BAYARD SMITH,   22d July, 1778.

On the part & behalf of the State of Delaware

THO. M'KEAN,   NICHOLAS VAN DYKE.
  Feby. 12, 1779.
JOHN DICKINSON,
  May 5th, 1779

On the part and behalf of the State of Maryland

JOHN HANSON,   DANIEL CARROLL,
  March 1, 1781.   Mar. 1, 1781.

On the part and behalf of the State of Virginia

RICHARD HENRY LEE, JNO. HARVIE,
JOHN BANISTER,   FRANCIS LIGHTFOOT LEE.
THOMAS ADAMS,

On the part and behalf of the State of No. Carolina

JOHN PENN,   CORNS. HARNETT,
  July 21st, 1778.   JNO. WILLIAMS.

On the part & behalf of the State of South Carolina

HENRY LAURENS,   RICHD. HUTSON,
WILLIAM HENRY DRAYTON, THOS. HEYWARD, Junr.
JNO. MATHEWS,

On the part & behalf of the State of Georgia

JNO. WALTON,   EDWD. TELFAIR,
  24th July, 1778.   EDWD. LANGWORTHY.

The Monroe Doctrine (1823)

The Monroe Doctrine is a statement about U.S. foreign policy prepared by John Quincy Adams, and presented by President James Monroe to the Congress on December 2, 1823. The goal of the doctrine was to prevent European involvement in Latin America's new republics.

Fellow citizens of the Senate and House of Representatives:

Many important subjects will claim your attention during the present session, of which I shall endeavor to give, in aid of your deliberations, a just idea in this communication. I undertake this duty with diffidence, from the vast extent of the interests on which I have to treat and of their great importance to every portion of our Union. I enter on it with zeal from a thorough conviction that there never was a period since the establishment of our revolution when, regarding the condition of the civilized world and its bearing on us, there was greater necessity for devotion in the public servants to their respective duties, or for virtue, patriotism, and union in our constituents.

Meeting in you a new Congress, I deem it proper to present this view of public affairs in greater detail than might otherwise be necessary. I do it, however, with peculiar satisfaction, from a knowledge that in this respect I shall comply more fully with the sound principles of our government. The people being with us exclusively the sovereign, it is indispensable that full information be laid before them on all important subjects, to enable them to exercise that high power with complete effect. If kept in the dark, they must be incompetent to it. We are all liable to error, and those who are engaged in the management of public affairs are more subject to excitement and to be led astray by their particular interests and passions than the great body of our constituents, who, living at home in the pursuit of their ordinary avocations, are calm but deeply interested spectators of events and of the conduct of those who are parties to them. To the people every department of the government and every individual in each are responsible, and the more full their information the better they can judge of the wisdom of the policy pursued and of the conduct of each in regard to it. From their dispassionate judgment much aid may always be obtained, while their approbation will form the greatest incentive and most gratifying reward for virtuous actions and the dread of their censure the best security against the abuse of their confidence. Their interests in all vital questions are the same, and the bond, by sentiment as well as by interest, will be proportionably strengthened as they are better informed of the real state of public affairs, especially in difficult conjunctures. It is by such knowledge that local prejudices and jealousies are surmounted, and that a national policy, extending its fostering care and protection to all the great interests of our Union, is formed and steadily adhered to. . . .

At the proposal of the Russian imperial government, made through the minister of the emperor residing here, a full power and instructions have been transmitted to the minister of the United States at St. Petersburg to arrange by amicable negotiation the respective rights and interests of the two nations on the northwest coast of this continent. A similar proposal had been made by his imperial Majesty to the government of Great Britain, which has likewise been acceded to. The government of the United States has been desirous by this friendly proceeding of manifesting the great value which they have invariably attached to the friendship of the emperor and their solicitude to cultivate the best understanding with his government. In the discussions to which this interest has given rise and in the arrangements by which they may terminate the occasion has been judged proper for asserting, as a principle in which the rights and interests of the United States are involved, that the American continents, by the free and independent condition which they have assumed and maintain, are henceforth not to be considered as subjects for future colonization by any European powers. . . .

It was stated at the commencement of the last session that a great effort was then making in Spain and Portugal to improve the condition of the people of those countries, and that it appeared to be conducted with extraordinary moderation. It need scarcely be remarked that the result has been so far very different from what was then anticipated. Of events in that quarter of the globe, with which we have so much intercourse and from which we derive our origin, we have always been anxious and interested spectators. The citizens of the United States cherish sentiments the most friendly in favor of the liberty and happiness of their fellow men on that side of the Atlantic. In the wars of the European powers in matters relating to themselves, we have never taken any part, nor does it comport with our policy so to do. It is only when our rights are invaded or seriously menaced that we resent injuries or make preparation for our defense. With the movements in this hemisphere we are of necessity more immediately connected, and by causes which must be obvious to all enlightened and impartial observers. The political system of the allied powers is essentially different in this respect from that of America. This difference proceeds from that which exists in their respective governments; and to the defense of our own, which has been achieved by the loss of so much blood and treasure, and matured by the wisdom of their most enlightened citizens, and under which we have enjoyed unexampled felicity, this whole nation is devoted. We owe it, therefore, to candor and to the amicable relations existing between the United States and those powers to declare that we should consider any attempt on their part to extend their system to any portion of this hemisphere as dangerous to our peace and safety. With the existing colonies or dependencies of any European power, we have not interfered and shall not interfere. But with the governments who have declared their independence and maintained it, and whose independence we have, on great consideration and on just principles, acknowledged, we could not view any interposition for the purpose of oppressing them, or controlling in any other manner their destiny, by any European power in any other light than as the manifestation of an unfriendly disposition toward the United States. In the war between those new governments and Spain, we declared our neutrality at the time of their recognition, and to this we have adhered, and shall continue to adhere, provided no change shall occur which, in the judgment of the competent authorities of this government, shall make a corresponding change on the part of the United States indispensable to their security.

The late events in Spain and Portugal show that Europe is still unsettled. Of this important fact no stronger proof can be adduced than that the allied powers should have thought it proper, on any principle satisfactory to themselves, to have interposed by force in the internal concerns of Spain. To what extent such interposition may be carried, on the same principle, is a question in which all independent powers whose governments differ from theirs are interested, even those most remote, and surely none more so than the United States. Our policy in regard to Europe, which was adopted at an early stage of the wars which have so long agitated that quarter of the globe, nevertheless remains the same, which is, not to interfere in the internal concerns of any of its powers; to consider the government *de facto* as the legitimate government for us; to cultivate friendly relations with it, and to preserve those relations by a frank, firm, and manly policy, meeting in all instances the just claims of every power, submitting to injuries from none. But in regard to those continents, circumstances are eminently and conspicuously different. It is impossible that the allied powers should extend their political system to any portion of either continent without endangering our peace and happiness; nor can anyone believe that our southern brethren, if left to themselves, would adopt it of their own accord. It is equally impossible, therefore, that we should behold such interposition in any form with indifference. If we look to the comparative strength and resources of Spain and those new governments, and their distance from each other, it must be obvious that she can never subdue them. It is still the true policy of the United States to leave the parties to themselves in the hope that other powers will pursue the same course.

Seneca Falls Declaration (1848)

The Seneca Falls Declaration, a "declaration of sentiments," was issued at an important women's rights convention held at Seneca Falls, New York in July, 1848. The convention was organized by Elizabeth Cady Stanton and Lucretia Mott.

We hold these truths to be self-evident; that all men and women are created equal; that they are endowed by their Creator with certain inalienable rights; that among these are life, liberty, and the pursuit of happiness; that to secure these rights governments are instituted, deriving their just powers from the consent of the governed. . . .

Now, in view of this entire disfranchisement of one-half the people of this country, their social and religious degradation, in view of the unjust laws above mentioned, and because women do feel themselves aggrieved, oppressed, and fraudulently deprived of their most sacred rights, we insist that they have immediate admission to all the rights and privileges which belong to them as citizens of the United States.

[Excerpt]

Emancipation Proclamation (1862)

President Abraham Lincoln issued the Emancipation Proclamation on September 23, 1862, in order to gain world support for the Union cause. The document stated that after January 1, 1863, all slaves in the rebel states would be free. The proclamation did not apply to the border states of Delaware, Kentucky, Maryland, and Missouri, nor to that part of the Confederacy already occupied by Northern troops, such as Tennessee and parts of Virginia and Louisiana.

By the President of the United States of America:
A PROCLAMATION

Whereas, on the twenty-second day of September, in the year of our Lord one thousand eight hundred and sixty-two, a proclamation was issued by the president of the United States, containing, among other things, the following, to wit:

"That on the first day of January, in the year of our Lord one thousand eight hundred and sixty-three, all persons held as slaves within any state or designated part of a state, the people whereof shall then be in rebellion against the United States, shall be then, thenceforward and forever, free; and the executive government of the United States, including the military and naval authority thereof, will recognize and maintain the freedom of such persons and will do no act or acts to repress such persons, or any of them, in any efforts they may make for their actual freedom.

"That the executive will, on the first day of January aforesaid, by proclamation, designate the states and parts of states, if any, in which the people thereof, respectively, shall then be in rebellion against the United States; and the fact that any state, or the people thereof, shall on that day be in good faith represented in the Congress of the United States, by members chosen thereto at elections wherein a majority of the qualified voters of such states shall have participated, shall, in the absence of strong countervailing testimony, be deemed conclusive evidence that such state, and the people thereof, are not then in rebellion against the United States."

Now, therefore, I, Abraham Lincoln, president of the United States, by virtue of the power in me vested as commander in chief of the army and navy of the United States, in time of actual armed rebellion against the authority and government of the United States, and as a fit and necessary war measure for suppressing said rebellion, do, on this first day of January, in the year of our Lord one thousand eight hundred and sixty-three, and in accordance with my purpose so to do, publicly proclaimed for the full period of one hundred days from the day first above mentioned, order and designate as the states and parts of states wherein the people thereof, respectively, are this day in rebellion against the United States, the following, to wit:

Arkansas, Texas, Louisiana (except the parishes of St. Bernard, Plaquemines, Jefferson, St. John, St. Charles, St. James, Ascension, Assumption, Terre Bonne, Lafourche, St. Mary, St. Martin, and Orleans, including the city of New Orleans), Mississippi, Alabama, Florida, Georgia, South Carolina, North Carolina, and Virginia (except the forty-eight counties designated as West Virginia, and also the counties of Berkeley, Accomac, Northampton, Elizabeth City, York, Princess Ann, and Norfolk, including the cities of Norfolk and Portsmouth), and which excepted parts are for the present left precisely as if this proclamation were not issued.

And by virtue of the power and for the purpose aforesaid, I do order and declare that all persons held as slaves within said designated states and parts of states are, and henceforward shall be, free; and that the executive government of the United States, including the military and naval authorities thereof, will recognize and maintain the freedom of said persons.

And I hereby enjoin upon the people so declared to be free to abstain from all violence, unless in necessary self-defense; and I recommend to them that, in all cases when allowed, they labor faithfully for reasonable wages.

And I further declare and make known that such persons, of suitable condition will be received into the armed service of the United States to garrison forts, positions, stations, and other places and to man vessels of all sorts in said service.

And upon this act, sincerely believed to be an act of justice, warranted by the Constitution upon military necessity, I invoke the considerate judgment of mankind and the gracious favor of Almighty God.

In witness whereof, I have hereunto set my hand and caused the seal of the United States to be affixed.

Done at the city of Washington this first day of January, in the year of our Lord one thousand eight hundred and sixty-three, and of the independence of the United States of America the eighty-seventh.

By the President:
William H. Seward,
Secretary of State.
Abraham Lincoln

The American's Creed (1917)

The American's Creed, composed by William Tyler Page in 1917, is a statement of our common political values. It is a set of beliefs about the proper role of government and the dignity of the individual. It attempts to show the consensus of Americans' values and beliefs. The values expressed are individualistic, democratic, and egalitarian.

Composed in 1917 by William Tyler Page (1868–1942).

"I believe in the United States of America as a government of the people, by the people, for the people; whose just powers are derived from the consent of the governed; a democracy in a Republic; a sovereign Nation of many sovereign States; a perfect Union, one and inseparable; established upon those principles of freedom, equality, justice, and humanity for which American patriots sacrificed their lives and fortunes.

"I therefore believe it is my duty to my country to love it; to support its Constitution; to obey its laws; to respect its flag; and to defend it against all enemies."

The Preamble to the Charter of the United Nations

Just as the United States is governed by the rules set forth in the Constitution, so too is the United Nations governed by the rules set forth in the Charter of the United Nations drafted and put into force in 1945. The U.N. Charter, like the Constitution, begins with a preamble that expresses the spirit of the organization.

We the peoples of the United Nations determined

> to save succeeding generations from the scourge of war, which twice in our lifetime has brought untold sorrow to mankind, and

> to reaffirm faith in fundamental human rights, in the dignity and worth of the human person, in the equal rights of men and women and of nations large and small, and

> to establish conditions under which justice and respect for the obligations arising from treaties and other sources of international law can be maintained, and

> to promote social progress and better standards of life in larger freedom,

and for these ends

> to practice tolerance and live together in peace with one another as good neighbors, and

> to unite our strength to maintain international peace and security, and

> to ensure, by the acceptance of principles and the institution of methods, that armed force shall not be used, save in the common interest, and

> to employ international machinery for the promotion of the economic and social advancement of all peoples,

have resolved to combine our efforts to accomplish these aims.

Accordingly, our respective governments, through representatives assembled in the city of San Francisco, who have exhibited their full powers found to be in good and due form, have agreed to the present Charter of the United Nations and do hereby establish an international organization to be known as the United Nations.

Notes

Notes

Notes

Notes